DEFENDING MARRIAGE:

Twelve Arguments for Sanity

DEFENDING MARRIAGE:

Twelve Arguments for Sanity

SAINT BENEDICT + PRESS
Charlotte, North Carolina

Cataloging-in-Publication data on file with the Library of Congress.

Typeset by Lapiz.

Cover artwork and design by Chris Pelicano.

ISBN: 978-1-61890-604-5

Published in the United States by
Saint Benedict Press, LLC
PO Box 410487
Charlotte, NC 28241
www.SaintBenedictPress.com

Printed and bound in the United States of America.

Contents

Prologue

I AM writing this book in gratitude to my father and mother, who introduced me to God and to the Church and to love.

In my mind's eye I see a photograph of my parents before I came into the world. They are relaxing on the beach at a local lake, one of those little picnic areas with a concession stand for hamburgers and fries, and an arcade with skee-ball and other games of skill and luck, and picnic tables, and plenty of ordinary people with their shouting troops of children.

In those days you didn't have to discern which lakes were good for children and which weren't, since every place except for a few of the taverns were for children, and people comported themselves accordingly. I never got the impression from my mother and father that such modesty implied any sacrifice or exercise of self-control. It was the natural expression of an innocence they had kept whole and hearty into their young adulthood.

That's not to say they were reserved or prudish. Far from it. It's hard to pretend to be the cool socialite when you are the children of hardscrabble Italian coal miners, when neither one of you could entertain any thought of college, and when you grew up in big families with only a couple of bedrooms and an outhouse. But there was my mother, a beauty in a one-piece bathing suit, and my father, all skinny muscle and bone, both of them dark from the sun. They were in love with one another.

I write those words—they were in love with one another—
and they should need no explanation. But I must explain
nevertheless. It's the whole scene at the lake that we must
remember. My father and mother didn't deliberate about it,
because they didn't have to. It was taken for granted; to be in
love, not just to feel the rush of infatuation, but really to love, is
not to see only the beloved and nothing else in the world, since
that's to turn the beloved into an idol, and no idol can bear the
weight of worship. The idol must collapse into disillusionment,
into rubble and dust. It is instead to see the love you share as
embracing the world, not bound by place and time, by chance
and change. It is to say, "All that I am is yours, now and forever."
The love of the married man and woman remembers the past
and opens itself in humility and gratitude to the future, in the
very act of its consummation. It binds together the generations.
In it we recall the children we were, and we bring the child into
our midst, born from our love.

My father and mother could not get married right away. He
had to serve in the army for two years first, and during that
time they hardly saw one another. She worked in a dress factory to support her parents, until her youngest sister graduated
from high school and could take her place. Then he had to find
a job that would pay well enough for them to begin a family.
They waited for three years, and during that time they did not
pretend that they were married. That is, they did not sin against
the family. They did not act in selfish uncharity against the children—those they would bear, and the other people's children
who were swimming and splashing that day at Chapman's Lake.

I've said that they had preserved the innocence of children.
They had also preserved the child's natural sense of the sacred.
I'm not talking here about the objects in a church. Imagine a
place most dear to you, because there you go in the fullness of
solitude, to collect yourself, to think, to contemplate, perhaps

simply to be. Imagine a secret garden, enclosed with hedges and vines, whose existence no one suspects, though within it are mazy paths and sudden springs and flowers that have no name. Or perhaps it is a rocky outcrop of a hill, barren of green except for the moss on the stones and the low-lying patches of blueberry and wintergreen. You don't bring other people to this place. It means too much for that. You couldn't bear it if they treated it as a paltry thing. But you know that you will someday bring *one person* there, the one who will love it also, but who will, in a mysterious way, change it, complete it, because you are not complete in yourself. You know you are not complete, because your sex instructs you in that plain fact every day of your life. It proclaims, "You are *for the other.*"

And yet that still does not comprehend the reality, when a man and a woman give themselves, *as man and woman*, to one another without reserve and forever. The garden is secret, but the marriage is public, and it must be so, and the evidence was all around my father and mother at the lake, noisy and happy and impossible to miss—the children, the little ones and the lanky ones and the sturdy adult ones and the gray haired ones. The love of the married man and woman is not a private romance, but a recapitulation of the love that brought them into being in the first place, and that love is what we all duly celebrate. It betokens our continuing in time, through children; it gives our distant ancestors and our distant descendants a place among us.

Did my parents *abstain from sex* before they were married? What an ugly expression it is, and misleading, too! They could no more abstain from "sex" than they could suspend the laws of gravity, as in a cartoon, and imagine themselves not-a-man and not-a-woman, or a half-man and half-woman, or what-ever nightmare of unreality one may prefer. My father was a man and my mother was a woman—even a little child would know that. Sex is what nature provided them with. Did they then "abstain" from uniting in the marital embrace? Once you call things by their proper names, the names that reveal their reality, you see that the question makes no sense. To do what married people do, while not being married—to engage in the marital act without matrimony—to do the child-making thing, while denying it in intent, is to contradict yourself. It is to tell a lie. What they "abstained" from was the pretense, the lie. It is like saying that they abstained from painting graffiti all over a priceless statue. It is like saying that they held their itching fingers back from uprooting the roses in the garden. It is like saying that they denied themselves the pleasure of amputating a finger or hand; that they spurned the delights of self-betrayal, rationalization, and ennui. It is like saying that they refused the enticement to grow feeble before their time.

Yes, I'm quite aware that the marital act is attended by great physical pleasure. All the more then should that pleasure be enjoyed at the right time, in the right way; just as one does not order a wedding cake for dessert unless there has been a wedding, or lavish presents on an irresponsible student who has failed his exams. My parents did not *abstain*; that's what an athlete might do with beer to shed a few pounds. My parents kept themselves pure and whole for one another—for the *other* in his or her sexual being—which implies openness to generations past and to come. They wanted joy, not pleasure on the cheap. They wanted a feast filled with guests with something real and good to feast about, and not something sickly in a brown bag. They wanted *more*, not less.

They went to the altar as children, free of the memory of having betrayed or having been betrayed, free of the disheartening fear that the mock-reality has come before the ceremony, free of any reason for guilt. They were far from the only people who did so, then. Eight weeks later, I was conceived.

I'm writing this book to help people return to the goodness of reality: the goodness of sexual being, *male and female for one another*. The proximate motive for the book is the move, mainly among the wealthy people of the West, bored with reality and indifferent to this goodness, to pretend that a man *can in fact* marry a man, or a woman a woman. Gentle or inattentive or morally compromised people may say, "Let them do as they please," but no denial of reality comes without a steep cost, especially the reality of something as profound and powerful as sex. I wish to help people recover a sense of what made that photograph of my mother and father possible—an innocent passion that we no longer know.

The following are twelve arguments against the notion that we can pretend that there is no such thing, really, as sex that is, that a marriage is even conceivable apart from a man and a woman. But my real aim lies beyond that. It's to reconsider all the sad mistakes we've already made, so that we may once again have a world in which families thrive, in which families and not amputated individuals or mass industries or metastatic bureaucracies determine what a culture is and what it is for; or rather, in which that all-time-embracing sexual love of man and woman in marriage makes possible the conditions for any genuine culture at all.

I have seen too much loneliness and unhappiness, too much chaos without and deadness of heart within, to pretend that the moral law that all people accepted until a few years ago, even if they sometimes fell afoul of it, does not still hold true, and does not still offer men and women their best chance for happiness in this life. We may obey it or not; but the penalty for disobedience isn't ours to determine, no more than if we leapt from a cliff, intending to fly by flapping our arms. Nature is not obliged to confirm our self-deceit.

First Argument

We Must Not Give the Sexual Revolution the Force of Irrevocable Law

IT'S a rustic scene, a sheep-shearing feast. The shepherd lads and lasses are dancing to a merry tune, but all eyes are on one couple in particular, the young mistress of the feast and the lad who is courting her. He is the prince of the realm, though the only people there who know it are the young lady herself, his father, and his father's most trusted counselor. Those last two have arrived at the party in disguise, to spy upon the prince, to see whether the rumors are true, that the boy has fallen in love with a mere shepherdess. She was herself born a princess, though neither she nor anybody present is aware of it.

The suspicious king and the old man, her foster father, look on. "She dances featly," says the king, who has been attracted by her beauty, her grace, and her purity even though he is there to protect the royal blood from any base alliance. The old shepherd replies:

> *So she does anything; though I report it,*
> *That should be silent. If young Doricles*
> *Do light upon her, she shall bring him that*
> *Which he not dreams of.*

What is the old man talking about? What will she bring to the lad who loves her so dearly? It cannot be anything she shares with other women, or even with the beasts. That requires no great flight of imagination. That is no object of wonder. If it were a modern playwright and not Shakespeare directing this scene from *The Winter's Tale*, we would be treated with stale jests about how Doricles is attempting to get the girl Perdita into bed, or how Perdita, like the cunning husband-huntress in *My Big Fat Greek Wedding*, is playing her cards right, leading the boy on little by little until finally she hooks him with a ferocious night of fornication.

But in fact Doricles is attempting no such thing. When, before the feast, Perdita expresses uneasiness at being dressed in such merry garb as was traditional for the mistress at the sheep-shearing, the lad comforts her, noting his own disguise as a shepherd swain, and recalling humorously that the gods themselves took on different shapes to pursue their loves. And yet

> *their transformations*
> *Were never for a piece of beauty rarer,*
> *Nor in a way so chaste, since my desires*
> *Run not before mine honor, nor my lusts*
> *Burn hotter than my faith.*

There we have it. When we watch these two young people dancing, so deeply in love that, as the old shepherd puts it, "there is not half a kiss to choose / Who loves another best," we are watching devotion and innocence together. The prince is a passionate young man—Shakespeare gives us ample evidence of that—and yet his *faith*, that is his fidelity, the complete surrender of his will to Perdita, burns even hotter than his natural physical desires.

The works of Shakespeare are filled with bawdy humor, yet he always holds up for our admiration the virtue of purity, and he never leaves unpunished sins against marriage and the family, whether they occur before or after the wedding. In fact, what makes this particular scene so powerful is precisely the tension between what the spying king wants to believe—that his son is a deceitful fool and the girl a conniving hussy—and what the playwright actually presents to us, a scene of incomparable youth and beauty, radiating forth from the goodness and the innocence of the boy and girl in love.

We'd be wrong to suppose that this is just a playwright's dream. Shakespeare holds up for us an ideal to aim for—but endows that ideal with the solid flesh and the soundly beating hearts of real people; indeed, for the moment, they are far more real than the stock comic figures of the jealous father and the bumptious rustics who are also partakers in the dance. The jaundiced man sees the whole world through the sour yellow of his own disposition. "He that is giddy thinks the world goes round"—if you cannot conceive of the power of purity, yours is the problem and not the virtue's. If you have spent many hours, each one duller than the last, poring over pornographic images of the sexes, you'll not be able to see Perdita and Doricles as anything other than engagers in the same old act: the Wife of Bath's "olde daunce," and she isn't speaking of a reel or a polka. You will miss the beauty of this moment. You will miss its very soul.

I am insisting upon this, because the sexual revolution has scorched us all, and has made it nearly impossible to understand the goodness of purity, in both its masculine and feminine embodiments. We can hardly believe that the virtue exists at all. Nor do we see the inner harmony between that virtue and others that we do still say we believe in, such as kindness, generosity, and loyalty.

It was not supposed to be this way.

"If you're not with the one you love," sang the rockers at the Woodstock festival, "love the one you're with."

"I'm with you," said a girl to a perfect stranger.

That's a snapshot from the so-called Summer of Love. It rained hard over that weekend, and the irresponsible and childish organizers of the festival hadn't prepared for that eventuality. No surprise, since they hadn't prepared for the crowds, either, so the concert degenerated into a vast, muddy, litter-strewn field smelling of human waste, with thousands of people wet and cold and hungry, so that the National Guard had to be brought in to nurse them.

Popular singers urged us to open our hearts to love, meaning a free and easy practice of sexual intercourse, without what were called "hangups." Modesty was decried as prudishness, and chastity ridiculed as impossible or hypocritical. It was as if mankind's long history of meditation on the difficulties of love, the sacrifices it requires, and the ease with which lust comes in fancy dress to pass itself off as the real thing, had been consigned to oblivion. It was, morally speaking, as if an entire culture should forget the use of the wheel and axle.

But lust is a cruel taskmaster. It must be so. I cannot be cruel to someone whose full humanity is present to me, whom I see not as a thing, but as a person of mysterious possibilities, someone in a web of real relationships, a brother or a husband or a son. The prerequisite for cruelty is reduction. I must replace the human being with an image that will stoke or sate my lust for anger or vengeance. "Off the pigs!" cried the radical demonstrators of those days, recommending the murder of policemen. It had to be *pigs*, not John or Matt or Vince, not the beloved son of an elderly couple of modest means living in Bensonhurst, the husband of a shy young woman named Molly, at home right now with a three-year-old boy in cowboy pajamas and a baby girl nursing at the breast.

Likewise, lust, the engine, the fuel, and the waste product of the sexual revolution, reduces. I don't mean simply that the lusted-for person becomes an object, like an item at the sexual bazaar, to be picked up for quick satisfaction. The effect is even more harmful than that. It reduces both the person so used and the person who uses. It is not animalistic, since that charge does an injustice to animals, which mate for the preservation of their species. The man in the grip of lust is both less and more than an animal, and therefore in a far worse state. He uses a narrow part of his mind, the calculative, to reckon up pleasures for his body or for some dark corner of his imagination. An animal cannot do that; what's more, an animal *would not* do that without turning into something worse than an animal, something evil.

Lust is a liar. Even to engage in the act, to make it exciting, one must pretend that it means everything, that one is giving oneself entirely, that one is actually feeling the passion that the muscular exertion of the body helps to simulate. But when the full giving of oneself is missing, then even in the midst of the surge of adrenalin the thought will come, "I am putting on an act." *Omne animal post coitum triste est*, went the old saying: every living thing after coitus feels sadness. In lust, it is not sadness so much as disillusionment, and a strange impatience with oneself and one's partner in the illusion.

Shakespeare instructs us again:

> *The expense of spirit in a waste of shame*
> *Is lust in action: and till action, lust*
> *Is perjured, murderous, bloody, full of blame,*
> *Savage, extreme, rude, cruel, not to trust;*
> *Enjoyed no sooner but despised straight;*
> *Past reason hunted; and no sooner had,*
> *Past reason hated, as a swallowed bait*
> *On purpose laid to make the taker mad:*
> *Mad in pursuit and in possession so;*
> *Had, having, and in quest to have, extreme;*

A bliss in proof, and proved, a very woe;
Before, a joy proposed; behind, a dream.
All this the world well knows; yet none knows well
To shun the heaven that leads men to this hell.

If not Shakespeare, then Spenser or Milton or Browning—name virtually any great poet or thinker before the last minute on the anthropological clock.

What if human sexuality is indeed rooted in the fullness of being male and being female, ordained to one another in wedded love, "loyal, just, and pure," as Milton says, the fount of "Relations dear, and all the charities / Of father, son, and brother"? If that is true, then the embrace of lust will imply a rejection of the meaning of wedded love, and will have its consequences for those other human relationships also.

The first reaction of the lust-corrupted to something like the dance of Doricles and Perdita is wistful longing for something lost, for the virtue that he sees, but no longer possesses. Next comes a disconcerting incomprehension—what can this be? Next comes belittlement, a deliberate attempt to tear the good thing down, to reveal what is "really" beneath, a reality that is as sordid and base as the imagination of the would-be exposer. Last comes sheer boredom. It doesn't take long to reach that final state. It didn't take long after the sexual revolution. What good was marriage?

Experimentation abounded: the so-called "open marriages," public intercourse, intercourse under the influence of drugs. A few of the experiments fizzled out, though they are now resurging, as witnessed by the sewer of websites devoted to "swingers." Divorce became as common as breathing. Whole networks of human relations were torn asunder; husband from wife, parents from children, aunts and uncles from their nephews and nieces, grandparents from grandchildren, cousins from one another;

all of that web of meaning and belonging, extending far into the past and future, untimely ripped, battered, or severed forever, to satisfy the "needs" (often lust-driven, and nearly always selfish) of the divorcing adults. And if lust rules, those needs must be insatiable. The object of lust is like a false food that satisfies the craving for a while but gives no nourishment. It is like the poison that Shakespeare alludes to in his sonnet: a bait that makes the man who takes it more ravenous than ever.

Since lust reduces, why should anybody be surprised by the explosion of pornography among us? If we treat one another as tools, as commodities, what prevents us from buying and selling the commodity? A hundred years ago, unless you lived in a large city, you'd have to go well out of your way to find dirty novels or a peep show. The technology has changed that, but so has lax resignation to the evil. In what they discuss and the salaciousness of their photos, the magazines women buy at the grocery store are as salacious as anything put out by Hugh Hefner in the 1950s. Millions of ten-year-old children now regularly see on the internet things that a whole small country full of people would not have seen over the course of a hundred years. Our children witness perversions of all kinds, and no one cares, because we have become a pornographic people, *even if we do not all gaze at the pictures.* That is because we accept the principle undergirding the pornography, which is that the pursuit of sexual gratification is a good thing, maybe the greatest good of all, and trumps all other considerations, such as the health of marriages generally, the welfare and innocence of children, the promotion of virtue, and the common good.

What honest observer of our situation dares to argue that the results have not been disastrous? We were told that the legalization of abortion would lead, paradoxically, to fewer abortions, and fewer instances of child abuse. Instead it led to far more abortions than even the opponents ever imagined, and it so cheapened infant life that child abuse spiked sharply upward. No one any longer is surprised to hear, on local television, of a child chained to his bed and allowed to starve in his own filth, or a baby bludgeoned to death by a boyfriend, with the mother as accomplice.

We were told that the legalization of contraceptive drugs would lead to fewer unwanted children, and fewer children born out of wedlock. Anyone with a passing familiarity with the human race should have known otherwise. By reducing the perceived "risk" of pregnancy, contraception removed from the young woman the most powerful natural weapon in her arsenal against male sexual aggression. She no longer had any pressing reason not to concede to the boyfriend's wishes. So she agreed; and we now have two of five children born out of wedlock. I will have more to say about what this situation means for young people who are trying to do the right thing by themselves, their parents, and the children they hope someday to have. The sexual chaos has touched every family in the nation. Who does not know at least one family whose children require an essay merely to describe who under their roof is related to whom, and how?

Some reckon up the losses from this revolution by percentages: of unwed mothers, of aborted pregnancies, of children growing up without a parent, usually the father. But numbers can never really capture the human reality. We are not grains of sand in an aggregate. We are intellectual beings, with minds capable of doing what nothing else we know can do—to apprehend all of being itself, and even to imagine things that have never been. A dog cannot misuse his sexual power, which is in any case severely limited to the moment. But when a human being misuses his sexual power, that power which implies a total surrender of the self, and which bridges generations past and to come, the harm is not momentary. Neither the good nor the evil we do can ever be so contained.

I will tell two stories of a death. One day I was lying in the preparatory room of a hospital, waiting for a procedure that we hoped would allow me to walk again, or even to sit and stand without excruciating pain. The procedure did not work—my healing turned out to be baffling and wonderful, but that is another story. While I was waiting, I could hear the sniffling of a young woman in the bed next to mine. She was in her twenties, a little soft-bodied but not pretty. She was also quite alone.

The nurse came to do her paperwork. She was kindly, in an efficient and impersonal way. She had to ask a few questions, to satisfy all righteousness. She asked the girl whether she was there of her own will.

"Nobody is forcing you to do this?"

"No."

"And what is the reason you wish to have your pregnancy terminated?"

There was a hitch in the girl's voice. "I have a two year old at home already. I just can't deal with another one." Her boyfriend, the father of the first child, had dumped her. The father of the second child was not in the picture at all. She was angry.

"That's all right," said the nurse, and proceeded to tell her who her doctor would be and what she could expect. "Do you have anybody to take you home after the procedure?"

"Yes, my brother is coming to pick me up."

Apparently that was all that the nurse needed to hear.

And this scene, banal and sordid and hardhearted, is repeated well over a million times every year in the United States. It would mean, in the small town where I grew up, two dozen abortions every year, when, in my mother's time, there were not more than two or three unwed mothers in a whole decade. The reason was simple. It wasn't that people in an earlier time were *by nature* more virtuous (they weren't), or that there was more effective contraception (there were only condoms, modestly effective at best, and if any druggist tried to sell them openly, that would have been the end of his business), or that there were abortions going on constantly but unknown to everyone. That last supposition is absurd. There is not a shred of evidence to support it. Besides, in a small town, nothing stays secret for long, and unless abortion then was the safest procedure known to the medical profession, there would have been too many chances for complications to arise, which would have cost the town's only doctor his license.

No, the reason that there were, in my mother's time, very few unwed mothers, let alone abortions, is cultural. Those were the years when it was taken for granted, by "liberals" and "conservatives" alike, that sexual activity was for marriage, and that boys who enticed girls into bed were little better than ruffians, doing themselves and the girls great harm, not to mention the child who might be conceived by the heedless and illicit union. My parents were not readers, but my mother did have one book that she prized, Fulton Sheen's *Life Is Worth Living*, with its chapter on the holiness of the sexes, male and female, and their coming together in matrimony. Bishop Sheen, with his trace of an Irish brogue, his immense philosophical and theological learning (which he wore lightly), his mingled earnestness and good humor, and his blackboard, was the most beloved television personality of those days. As I say, a different culture.

"Had it been then," say those who cling, against all the evidence, to the myth of sexual liberation, "the girl in the hospital would have been a girl in a back alley, seeing a butcher." It isn't true. We are not speaking here of certainties but of overwhelming probabilities. There is no way to hide that many deaths. The butchers would have had to be the most skilled surgeons in the country, and the whole nation would have had to engage in a massive conspiracy of ignorance, and the same women then who believed that fornication was wrong would have almost all of them chosen to end their children's lives, and that at a time when doctors across the political spectrum were saying the simple truth, that human life begins at conception. Indeed, abortion proponents at that time, trying to soften the general animus against it, said that the procedure was quite safe, since it was usually performed within the bounds of the state law in question, by a doctor with access to anesthesia, antisepsis, and antibiotics.

No, had it been then, as far as it is possible for us to speak with confidence about anything in this world, that girl would have been married. "I don't know what I'm going to do," she says to the nurse, "with little Bobby hanging on my skirts all day long! But I tell you, all that big Bobby has to do is wink at me, and here I am."

I'm not assuming any great saintliness in this young woman, just a very ordinary measure of self-respect, honor, duty, and reverence for the goodness of man and woman in their immemorial embrace, and for the children that the embrace brings into the world. I'm describing most of the women of my mother's generation.

But there lay the mother yet not-a-mother in the curtained cell beside mine, alone, betrayed by the first father, betrayed by the second, betrayed by a callous hedonistic culture, betrayed by her own weakness, sniffling still after the nurse left her. Then she called her brother on her telephone, and there was iron in her voice. Her child that afternoon must die. But something must already have died within her and within us all to bring her to that pass.

Then there was the winter day in 1991 when I was called home. My father was going to die that day. He'd been suffering from liver cancer, and the organ had shut down, and his body was filled with the toxins. He hadn't been able to eat for several days, and now he could no longer drink. He was in his home, in his chair in the living room. It was now a matter of hours.

He'd doze a little now and then, but for the most part he was conscious and alert. He could hardly speak, but he did tell my brother and me to shovel the snow out of the driveway, because he knew that people might be stopping in. That they did. They were my aunts and uncles and cousins, our blood. One cousin leaned over his chair and spoke softly into his ear, reminiscing about the days when my father was his baseball coach, and laughing about something my father had said or done to straighten him out. We could hardly speak for gratitude.

When the crisis came and his breath began to rattle, we gathered round him, his wife and his four children. We told him we loved him. But in the last moment, he had eyes for one person alone. He turned towards my mother, his eyes very wide, as if he'd gone blind and were staring hard to find her face. He tried to whisper, so she bent her ear towards his lips.

"I love you," he said, and they were his last words on earth.

He had never known any other woman, and she had never known any other man.

The world after the sexual revolution is not entirely love-less; no world can be, so long as there are human beings in it. But love is not its natural growth. For the love of man and woman is necessarily oriented towards the gift of all, forever; that is required by the time-transcending and self-transcending sorts of creatures we are. And the sexual revolution denies that. It attacks that love at the root.

And what does this have to do with the pretense that a man *can* marry another man? That supposition, which never occurred to anybody until quite recently, is possible *only* among the rubble left by the sexual revolution. It is one of the fruits of that revolution. To reject the revolution is to reject what depends upon it and what cannot even be imagined without it. We cannot have things both ways. We cannot have a culture of marriage and family and a pseudoculture of divorce and abortion; that is a contradiction. We cannot have a culture of marriage and family and a pseudoculture of indifference with regard to male and female, and children "chosen" (or not) as accessories to their parents' lives; that is another contradiction. We cannot have a culture in which purity is held up as an ideal and a pseudoculture of pornography, sexual "experimentation" (note the coldly clinical term), and salaciousness celebrated as "edgy" and "bold"; that is still another contradiction.

It is time to rebuild among the ruins. We cannot begin to rebuild, though, if we assume that it is all right to wield the sledge hammers that brought the ruin in the first place.

Second Argument

We Must Not Enshrine in Law the Principle That Sexual Gratification Is a Personal Matter Only, with Which the Society Has Nothing to Do

IT'S hard for us to imagine, in a world of mass entertainment and its homogenization of peoples, how central an event the marriage is in every culture. It marks the most joyful celebration of a people, who see their renewal in the vows made by the young man and the young woman. For although marriage focuses upon the couple, it does so because they embody a rejuvenation in which everyone, young and old, male and female, takes part.

In his *Epithalamion*, the English Renaissance poet Edmund Spenser summons everyone in the neighborhood to the celebration of his wedding, even the nymphs of the Irish forests and the gods of the Irish streams—and after the priest has "knit the knot that ever shall remain," and the revelers have splashed themselves and the groom's walls with wine, and the girls have danced and the boys have run shouting up and down the street, and the hours of celebration have been hastened along in bonfires and glee, he bids everyone to leave him and his bride alone. There is a time for the public joy; actually almost seventeen hours of it, since Spenser jestingly says he's chosen just the wrong day of the year for his wedding, "Barnaby the bright," the summer solstice! But however long the day, eventually the sun will set and the sweet night will come. Then comes the time for private joy. Husband and wife enjoy each other's love, and pray that from their "timely seed" they may raise a large posterity.

Here we have an understanding of marriage far more profound than ours, which has been so desiccated that now it represents little more than the expression of two private acts of the will. But where does that profundity come from? Why is it not merely baroque fancy-work, when Spenser invokes the birds of the countryside? Let us listen:

> *Hark how the cheerful Birds do chant their Lays,*
> *And carol of Love's Praise.*
> *The merry Lark her Matins sings aloft,*
> *The Thrush replies, the Mavis descant plays,*
> *The Ouzel shrills, the Ruddock warbles soft;*
> *So goodly all agree, with sweet consent,*
> *To this Day's Merriment.*
> *Ah! my dear Love, why do ye sleep thus long,*
> *When meeter were that ye should now awake,*
> *T' await the coming of your joyous Make,*
> *And hearken to the Birds love-learned Song,*
> *The dewy Leaves among?*
> *For they of Joy and Pleasance to you sing,*
> *That all the Woods them answer, and their Echo ring.*

It is an immemorial tradition to see the love of man and woman in the context of the fruitfulness of nature. We find it in all of the great poets going back to the Greeks. It came to be traditional, though, only because it is natural and true.

The flowers, the fruit, the special foods, the fire, the singing, all show the marriage as springing from the goodness of the life around us. The birds really do carol the praise of love—that is what Mr. Cardinal is doing perched in the budding maple tree in March, attracting to his bravura the affection of Mrs. Cardinal, as they build their nest and mate and then bring food to their young. We preserve the notion when we say that a young wife carrying her first child is "nesting," preparing the house to be just right for the arrival of the child that will make her and her husband into a family.

What about the other creatures invited to the wedding—the people of the village? Man, says Aristotle, is that kind of creature who thrives best only in the context of a free, self-governing community. We need one another. People not so long ago had daily and evident proof of this. You could not go through a day without relying upon a web of personal relationships. There was the miller who ground your corn, the carter who carried your produce, the butcher who slaughtered your pig, the smith who shod your horse, the wheelwright who repaired your carriage. But people also depended upon one another for the sweeter things in life, for song, for worship, for conversation and the life of the mind, and for publicly determined decisions for securing the common good.

Now, the community, in its political organization, is not *interested* in a private friendship. That is, the community may provide the context in which such a friendship may flourish, but it is nothing for the community as such either to recognize or to celebrate. You don't register your bowling partner with the town clerk. That is not the case with marriage. We are all *interested* in marriage, that is, we all have a stake in it, because through marriage, or through actions that should have been performed within the haven of marriage, we have all come into being. It isn't simply a reflex of the emotions of the man and woman. It is the act of renewal. It brings together this family of blood relations with that family of blood relations, natural relations, the kinfolk that lay just claims upon us because we and they share some of the same history, the same cousins, even the same eyes and ears and noses. A marriage marries families, and it is the family, and not the abstracted autonomous individual, that is the foundation for the community.

In other words, were it not for children, there would be no reason for weddings at all, since there is no reason for the community to take note of whether John and Mike or any two unmarriageable people have been arguing lately or have patched up their differences, regardless of any behavior they may be indulging in when the doors are closed. But the community does have a powerful interest in what used to be called "public morals," since these impinge upon the welfare of the family, and thus upon the community's health and survival. It is precisely because the marital act is a child-making act that the community not only *may* protect it by the fencing of law and custom; it has a duty to do so, to protect itself and the most vulnerable of its members.

None of what I've just said would have been controversial, within living memory. It would not have been regarded as particularly liberal or conservative. Woodrow Wilson, the self-styled progressive, believed in those principles as earnestly as did the cautious William McKinley, who made certain every day that he waved from his office window to his invalid wife Ida, whom that hard-favored man loved most dearly. It's only now, when people do not know their neighbors and community life is as withered as a leaf in November, that we have come up with the strange notion that sexual activity is strictly a private affair. It cannot be; and children are the walking and talking proof of it. Consider the one thing we all have in common: we have all had a mother and a father; and the one thing that all societies at all stages of technological development have celebrated as betokening their survival: marriage with child-bearing; and the one thing that even a college professor can know as well as a boy growing up on a farm: that sexual congress is what binds it all together.

Some people will say, "But the family has *evolved*," thinking to shut down argument and to detach the family from biology by the use of a term derived, ironically, from biology itself. There are several obvious answers to this objection. The first is that it is not true. Ten thousand years ago, men married women and had children. In every society known to man, at all stages of technological development, among people who fly in airplanes and people who don't even use the wheel, men marry women and have children. In the single, small counterexample that I know of, the natives are said not to know where children come from, or so the anthropologists say, although natives do take delight in fooling anthropologists. In this tight little tribe, men do not marry women; but I daresay no one will hold them up as beacons of social, intellectual, and moral enlightenment.

What then can it mean to say that the family has *evolved*? If it means that the conditions in which families must live have changed, and that these conditions have attenuated the bonds between the generations and among members of the extended family, then I admit that this is so. But to the extent that the changed conditions are relevant, they testify *against* those who propose that we can detach the family completely from biology, as I shall show. In the main, they aren't relevant at all. Something may change in attendant conditions, but not in essence, and even if those conditions are quite significant, it does not mean that the thing itself has changed at all. A family made up of a father, a mother, and two children, none of whom speak to one another except when watching television, all four of them well-jowled and living at their ease, is in some sense not the same as a family of peasant farmers, a father and mother and ten children, scratching a life out of the land, and intimate with the droll music of one another's snores as they snug up together in a two-bedroom house. But as poor as the rich family is, and as rich as the poor family is, they are both still families. A dog with a missing leg is still a dog. A cat without his claws is still a cat.

Return to that verb, *evolve*. Its inner meaning is to unfold ever greater and more powerful potentialities that had lain latent within. So a seed germinates and develops into a seedling, which then unfolds in trunk and limbs and leaves and becomes a tree. A small settlement of coal prospectors huddled in the hills begins to grow when they find a rich substrate, and soon there are not only miners but grocers and millers, and then a spur of a railroad, and then a foundry, and after a generation or so the settlement is an incorporated town. This I would call an *evolution*, in the common sense of that word.

So then, has the family *evolved*? By what common-sense criterion? Is it healthier than ever? Is divorce almost unknown? Are almost all children born within the stable haven of the unshakeable vows of matrimony? Does the individual family possess a wider zone of autonomy and authority than before? Is the family more determinative in the progress of the municipality, the state, and the nation? Is the family more culturally productive—so that we have more and more families like the artists Bellini in Venice and della Robbia in Florence, and the musical Bach family in Leipzig, and the great violin-making Amati and Stradivari families? Do people acknowledge subservience to the family—doctors, teachers, and politicians especially? Is the family, I say, now something mightier than it was, as the tall oak is mightier than the sapling it used to be?

Has it not been disintegrating—not *evolving*, but collapsing? Is it not punier and weaker than before? Certainly smaller! Are not the unions of men and women, many of whom do not bother to marry before conceiving a child, more tenuous than ever? Is there a single facet of contemporary life in which the family is not subject to intrusion and overrule, by social workers, school teachers, and doctors? Are not the "blended" families and step-families and other disorganizations rather like a garden of weeds and uprooted flowers, in which everything but dependability rules? In what sphere does this brave new family govern? What great things has it built, economically and socially?

The sexual drive is the most powerful among our animal motives, most dynamic when well governed, and most destructive when it is not. It's absurd to say that the public, by custom and by laws that flow from those customs and sustain them in turn, should have no right to guide the single thing most determinative of what kind of culture they will live in, if any culture at all. It's a contradiction in terms, as if one were to say on Monday that people have a right to political action, and then on Tuesday remove from their purview what touches them most intimately, and what all adults of ordinary intelligence can be expected to know a great deal about. We believe that Jack the barber can cast a vote for a congressman based on his understanding of international trade, of which very few people are in a position to know much, but *not* on his understanding of what makes for strong families and healthy neighborhoods. Thus does rule by "experts" masquerade as democracy.

Until the sexual revolution, most people understood that customs and laws regarding sex were customs and laws to strengthen or at least to protect the family, and that the family was not something created by the State, but was its own small kingdom, a natural society, founded in the bodily nature of man. Any of the popes since Leo XIII may be cited to this effect, but since my contemporaries are allergic to them, I will cite instead one member of a group of seven liberal and "progressive" signatories to a series of articles called "Present-Day Papers," published in *Century Magazine*, 1889–1890. His name was William Chauncy Langdon, one of the earliest promoters in America of the Young Men's Christian Association, which in those days was not a day-care center and gymnasium for middle class women, but a training ground for young men, to strengthen body and mind and help them to become productive and virtuous citizens.

We need, says Langdon, "a searching revision of our shallow, individualistic, popular conceptions of the family." Note that well. Langdon sees a shallow individualism as the *enemy* of the family—not as the protector of the family and an enemy to the leviathan State, as self-styled conservatives among us would claim; and not as the guarantor of a healthy "diversity," as self-styled progressives among us would claim. Society "is made up not merely of so many men, women, and children, but rather of so many families." If the State is less than the human as to being, the detached individual is thwarted from realizing the fullness of his being: "The single person is not a social unit, but rather a constituent member of an actual, or a potential, or a frustrated family."

To see that truth is to see a panorama of ills consequent upon its rejection. Langdon knows that when he asserts the primacy of the family, he sets himself against a host of social movements whose proponents may little realize that they are marching under one banner:

> Any low ideas of marriage, any [permissive] divorce legislation, any factitious claims for "women's rights," any narrow or perverted conception of education, or any abnormal conditions of living forced upon the working classes—any of these which tend practically to segregate the sexes one from the other, to relieve either from the mutual dependence which should unite them,

to create distinct, and it may be antagonistic, interests, to weaken the sense of joint responsibility, or to make the home impossible, are essentially destructive and anarchic in their character; for the moral dissolution of the family would sap the very foundations of all social order alike in state and church.

That's a statement of astonishing breadth and insight. He is not referring to separate schools for girls and boys, but to the evil root of sexual individualism, which comes in various guises. One such is to see the woman's interest as segregated from, or at odds with, the man's. Hence we have programs in "women's studies," a monstrous absurdity, as if one were to study only the left side of the body. And that evil root is akin to the evil root of rapacious industrialism, which narrows or perverts the education of workers, or herds them into tenements and hangs them with debt to the company store. It is also akin to the evil root of sexual permissiveness, which replaces self-control and fidelity with self-indulgence and willfulness. A "debased public opinion," vitiated by bad law and "trashy literature, virtually assumes that marriage, if not a mere civil contract, is at all events a relation to be determined solely by mutual inclination or convenience." Read that sentence carefully. Langdon sees that sexual laissez-faire causes the marriage to degenerate into a "mere civil contract," one which, nowadays, is less binding than a business partnership. That is because what is based upon inclination and convenience, and not the nature of man and his duties towards his ancestors, his children, and his fellow men, will fall when the inclination fades and circumstances change.

One might expect a nation of sexual individualists to educate children to go their own bold ways; but that cannot be, because there is no fully realized human individual apart from a family. So, paradoxically, such a nation leans towards banishing the family from rightful authority over the schools, which then become standardized, like factories. "Sparta," says Langdon, expecting us to understand his allusion to a totalitarian regime which seized boys from their homes to live in barracks, "presents to us no illustration of an educational philosophy for a Christian people." Real education is of persons made in the image of God, and cannot be effected "by contract or in the aggregate. In the family alone, and by or on the immediate responsibility of those parents by whom were imposed upon each child from before its birth the physical, mental, and spiritual conditions on which all true after education must be based, can an ideal early education be conducted." Schools and schoolteachers there may be, but they must "be regarded only as the representative deputy or the substitute for the family."

Let's pause here to consider the point he has made. It is strange to us only because we have come to take mass education, impersonally applied to so many millions of children as caps are applied to bottles on an assembly line, for granted. When a man and a woman come together in marriage and conceive a child, they stamp him, as it were, with "the physical, mental, and spiritual conditions on which all true after education must be based." Man has always known this to be true, long before we discovered the specifics of genetics. Musical talent, a flair for painting, linguistic facility, craft in the hands—countless are the ways in which a child can resemble his father, his mother, his brothers and sisters, his cousins, his grandparents, his aunts and uncles, and anyone else in the flock of the family. The child enters the world among people who are like him, and whose ways provide for him a little world in which to develop the singular array of talents and interests he has inherited from them. He is unique in his own being, but that uniqueness comes to him in relation to others who are close to him, and with whom he unites as a member of a family in relation to other and different families.

If the family directs the education of the child, that education will be *for the child as a member of the family*, and of a future family of his own, for "neither is the man without the woman, neither the woman without the man, in the Lord." It will respect the "complementary characteristics" of boys and girls, not that the sexes might be segregated as in Sparta, but that they may be more firmly united in marriage. "Certainly a merely political philosophy of education," says Langdon, and here our right and left are indistinguishable, "must logically result in the social obliteration of sex, in the gravest wrongs to women, called in grimmest sarcasm her rights, and, in the last analysis—were it possible—in the moral elimination of the family." Consider the hard-won right of a woman to be blown to bits on the battlefield, or to drudge forty hours a week for people she does not love, scraping the plaque off their teeth or shuffling and filing paper after paper, or to raise a child without benefit of wedlock, or to pave a highway from Washington into the living rooms of her sisters—individualism and a vast governmental apparatus marching together, and the family, or what is left of it, a sickly thing that cannot manage to instruct children in virtue, much less lead a community or a nation.

Langdon sees that all these things are related. We cannot talk about sex without talking about the relations of man and woman in marriage. We cannot talk about those relations without talking about the health and the power and the range of influence of the family. We cannot talk about the family without talking about the education of children which properly belongs to the family. We cannot talk about that education without talking about the preservation and propagation of the child's family into succeeding generations. All of these issues bear directly upon the health of the State, as our swollen welfare rolls and our shameful rates of incarceration amply show. To say that the individual's supposed need for sexual gratification, in what manner and under what circumstances he alone is to determine, trumps all other considerations, or is strictly personal, is plain madness, and madness of a sort that no previous society had the wealth or the temerity to countenance.

C. S. Lewis illustrated by an analogy the absurdity of this idolatry of sex. Suppose someone were to say, "No man can possibly lead a fully human life unless he enjoys great games of golf." We would properly look upon him as insane. He would be elevating a minor pleasure to the apex of human existence. He would also be isolating it from all other human concerns. The Lord of the Birdie must have his burnt offerings, and only afterwards come considerations of beauty and virtue and the common good. You enter the drug store and see the headlines blaring at you from the magazines, "Hot New Golf Tips!" "What Your Pro Isn't Telling You!" "Long Clubs for Long Hitters!" "Amazing Holds for Putters!" And you see people gazing at photos of professional golfers, open mouthed, lost to the world.

The madness there isn't just that golf happens not to excite such stupid fascination, but that it does not merit that stupid fascination, and neither does the copulative action we have in common with the beasts. What does merit honor is the *marital* act, which is not merely copulative, which far transcends inclination and convenience, which is oriented toward new being, which is therefore open to generations past and to come, and which is family-making, with the family not a small set of people who happen to live under one roof, but a natural society, founded in biological fact.

We see then that the principle of sexual autonomy is fundamentally antisocial. It not only retreats from social responsibility; it breeds social irresponsibility. Let's suppose that we treated business decisions with the same cavalier indifference with which we treat the exercise of the sexual powers. Suppose a young person could start a "business" on a whim, when he "felt he was ready," amassing debt to various creditors, and then, having had neither the intention nor the capacity to create a working concern, declare bankruptcy without impinging upon his credit, stiffing the creditors, and earning for his errors a healthy dole from the federal government. There would still be plenty of genuine businesses in the upper classes, but a young man setting forth to create one, unless he already possessed the advantages of class—money, and a pedigree from a good college—would be automatically *immiserated*. He would find himself struggling, for no apparent material reward, without good prospects for success in an environment so corrupt, and without *any moral support from his society*. He would likely sweat himself to death for nothing, not even a pat on the back from his social "betters." He'd be playing the part of a sucker in a game rigged in every way against his industriousness and honesty. There are nations in this world in which those conditions obtain, and the result is political dysfunction and a gulf between rich and poor, in manner of life far more than even in income.

It wasn't the lower classes that preached the religion of sexual liberation. That came from the upper classes, with their comfortable cushions against the resulting disorder. What did it matter to them that they were polluting the waters? Their houses were upstream. The biological absurdism of same-sex pseudogamy (mock-marriage) is just the latest effort of the same irresponsible destroyers.

Let those who are in favor of the world that the sexual revolution has produced defend it on its "merits," and not decree all discussion out of bounds from the beginning. We are not talking about privacy here, but about the air we all must breathe and the water we all must drink.

Third Argument

We Should Not Drive a Deeper Wedge between Men and Women

I'VE said that matrimony bridges the gap between generations past and to come, while uniting families in the warm
and vital relationships of blood. It does so in hope that the children will be born within those bonds of love.

But we could not have children without a bridge thrown
over a more dangerous divide, that which separates two groups
of human beings who seldom understand one another, whose
bodies and psyches are so markedly different, who try to love
one another, and so often fail, yet who try again for all that.
I mean men and women. The wedding is a symbol of the union
of differences.

I am looking at an illustration by Norman Rockwell, called
"First Love." It graced a cover for the *Saturday Evening Post*
in 1926. It would not grace any of our magazine covers now,
because we no longer prize the innocence and the love that it
celebrates, with good humor and sympathy. A boy and a girl are
sitting on a makeshift bench, with their backs to us. He's got a
mop of red hair and is clearly a bit taller than she is. He's sitting
bolt upright, with bandanas sticking out of his back pockets. His
shirt sleeves are rolled up over his elbows, and his right arm, a

skinny but sturdy boy's arm, embraces her around the waist. She's leaning his way, her head tilted so as to rest, a little awkwardly, upon his shoulder, with her pigtails sticking out. She's wearing a blue skirt with lighter blue polka dots. He's wearing a light blue shirt and blue suspenders, with a blue check pattern in the trousers. The clothing suggests that the boy and the girl are different, and at the same time that because of those very differences they are *for one another.*

She's holding a couple of daisies in her free hand on the right. Evidently the boy has given them to her as a token of his love; it means that he thinks she is pretty, like the daisies. He's had to go forth from himself to do this, and we see it by what Rockwell places in the foreground: a fishing rod and bobber, laid carelessly upon the ground; an open can of bait, with one worm sneaking his way out; and a despondent beagle, disappointed in his hopes for a blissful day at the fishing hole. The chance for that day has come and gone, because boy and girl are gazing up at the great full moon rising beyond them.

Everything about that scene is healthy and normal and right.

When I was seven years old, the cousins of my cousins moved into the neighborhood, and one of them was a slender little girl of my age. Though she was a little bit of a tomboy too, and played wiffle ball with us, she was also sweet and girlish. She set up a big concession stand in front of her house, across the street from our small playground, where she sold lemonade and cookies and candy. I thought the store was terrific. When her birthday came, her grandparents were in from Germany to join the celebration, and I was invited. I dressed up in a jacket and tie. The girl was wearing a dress. When the grownups played German waltz music on the record player, she and I danced—I'm supposing that either we had seen how it was done or that her parents helped us out, because there's a photograph of me with an arm upon her waist, her hand upon my shoulder, and our free hands together, arms extended.

No doubt we stumbled about, but what made the grownups encourage us to dance? It was healthy and normal and right, that's what.

A few years later, meddlesome state officials ordered the nuns at my school to set aside time every week for "physical education." The irony is that the school had long given us an entire hour for lunch, so that after ten minutes of gobbling, the kids spent the next fifty running around outside. That's those who brought their lunches to school. The others rushed home for lunch and then rushed back to get some playing time in before the one o'clock bell. Most of the students also walked to and from the school, so that too allowed for a school day that was much shorter than the one the public school students had to endure. But we had to abide by the law, so the sisters conceived of a remarkable plan, which would have worked a great deal better in any other age but our own. They hired a dance instructor.

In any other age, that would have meant boys dancing with girls, all the time. Because this was the late sixties, it meant that we engaged in spasmodic jerks across the dance floor about half of the time, with a "partner" of the opposite sex, and that boys really danced with girls the rest of the time. We learned the polka and the waltz and the reel and a few other genuine dances which I soon forgot, because outside of the little greenhouse of my school those folkways were being abandoned, and nobody knew how to do anything.

Why did the sisters hire somebody to teach the boys to dance with the girls? They were not prudes, nor were they corrupted in their imaginations. They were guiding our imaginations, and building up what would have been good habits in us, had those habits been at all confirmed by the broader culture around us. It was healthy and normal and right.

It's a mark of our confusion that we should need to be reminded of these things, or even persuaded of them—as if we could forget that small children need their mothers! But we have forgotten that, too, or we have vigorously attempted to thrust it from our consciousness. Yet nature is what nature is. Small children need their mothers. Boys are for girls, and girls are for boys.

The customs of every healthy culture bear it out. When a lad in Sweden courted the girl he loved, he would build for her a beautiful wooden chest for her clothing and her linens, carving the wood by hand, and decorating it with folk painting. Thus arose a genial competition among the boys, to see who could fashion the best piece of furniture. It was a boyish token of love. It declared, "I have skill, I can support you and the children we will have, I'm not afraid of hard work," and, most important, "You are all the world to me, and as lovely as I have tried to make this chest, you are lovelier still." When a lad in Austria courted the girl he loved, he would climb into the mountains to bring her back the delicate flowers of the edelweiss, which grew in dangerous places, on the brows of cliffs. It declared, "I am brave, I can support you and the children we will have, I'll give my all to you," and, most important, "You are lovelier than this most precious of our flowers."

Notice that the sexes here are not interchangeable. We'd find it improper and strangely humiliating if Austrian boys were to keep themselves aloof in their rooms until the girls who loved them scrabbled their way up the alpine escarpments to gather some edelweiss. That's not because of some arbitrary custom. It is because of the bodies of men and women, both as they are in themselves and as they are for one another; those bodies are what give rise to the custom and to others like it. The custom was but a manifestation of a healthy nature.

The girl's body is made for childbearing and for nursing and caring for children. It is stamped upon her so obviously

that only people perversely determined to be blind can miss it.
We see it in her breasts, the prominence of her hips, the softness
of her skin, the sleekness of her hair, the childlike pitch of her
voice, her small hands and slender fingers, her gentle chin, her
eyes that well so easily with tears (that's a physiological fact),
and the sudden shifts in her mood, betokening ferocity if she
and her children should be unjustly put upon or threatened.
She is a hundred things a man is not, and he knows it well. So
says the still sinless Adam to the angel Raphael in *Paradise Lost:*

> *When I approach*
> *Her loveliness, so absolute she seems*
> *And in herself complete, so well to know*
> *Her own, that what she wills to do or say,*
> *Seems wisest, virtuousest, discreetest, best;*
> *All higher knowledge in her presence falls*
> *Degraded, Wisdom in discourse with her*
> *Loses discountenanced, and like folly shows;*
> *Authority and Reason on her wait,*
> *As one intended first, not after made*
> *Occasionally; and to consummate all,*
> *Greatness of mind and nobleness their seat*
> *Build in her loveliest, and create an awe*
> *About her, as a guard Angelic placed.*

The angel will warn Adam not to place overmuch value on
the superficialities of a woman's beauty, but there is nothing in
Adam's praise of Eve that is itself wrong. Eve was indeed *intended
first*, that is, not an afterthought in God's plan, but intended to
be Adam's helpmate from the beginning. In the innocent soul
of Eve, whom Milton causes us, before the first sin, to regard
as a queen, there is indeed magnanimity and nobility, and,
enthroned in such beauty, they do inspire awe—like an angelic
guard placed before holy ground.

I believe that there are still some men here and there who understand what Adam is talking about. Boys should be encouraged to think of girls with the same deference and honor; and not as sexual playmates who happen to be equipped with different tools, or as just-boys, only shorter and weaker. And what of those boys? Their masculinity too is stamped upon their bodies. They are taller than their sisters, with broader shoulders and heavier bones. Their skin and hair are rougher, their voices deeper, and the hair that grows on their chins marks them out as children no more. They have more blood in their veins, and more iron in the blood. Even a little boy, if he is at all active, has the man's body shadowed forth in miniature, in the narrowness of the waist, the sturdy shoulders, and the indentations on the back and the arms and the chest that give promise of strength. Just as man seeks in woman what he does not possess in himself, so woman seeks in man what she does not possess in herself.

So we have Eve's appreciation for Adam. The nobility of a good man hasn't been the inspiration for female writers and artists as has been, for men, the beauty and grace of a good woman. Yet Milton's Eve, telling us of how she saw Adam for the first time and how she shied away from him because he was not so fair, not so "winning soft" as her own image she had seen in the water, also praises Adam for courting her and for winning her over:

> *Thou following cried'st aloud, "Return fair Eve,*
> *Whom fli'st thou? whom thou fli'st, of him thou art,*
> *His flesh, his bone; to give thee being I lent*
> *Out of my side to thee, nearest my heart*
> *Substantial Life, to have thee by my side*
> *Henceforth an individual solace dear;*
> *Part of my soul I seek thee, and thee claim*

My other half." With that thy gentle hand
Seized mine, I yielded, and from that time see
How beauty is excelled by manly grace,
And wisdom, which alone is truly fair.

At which she leans upon his naked bosom, her long curly tresses half hiding her breast pressing against his, and he kisses her "with kisses pure," while Satan leers at them from the bushes, attracted to what he sees despite himself, and hating it all the more because it is innocent, and it is love. Says he:

Sight hateful, sight tormenting! Thus these two,
Imparadised in one another's arms,
The happier Eden, shall enjoy their fill
Of bliss on bliss, while I to Hell am thrust,
Where neither joy nor love, but fierce desire,
Among our other torments not the least,
Still unfulfilled with pain of longing pines.

Before the sexual revolution, women really did understand and value the manhood that moves Eve to lean the closer to Adam, and they understood too that anyone who would sneer at such manhood could not possibly be friendly to their womanhood, either. Rich people can afford a yacht full of vice, and for a generation or two they can appear to have gotten away with it, gleaming on the surface while rotting within. Poor people, or even people of ordinary means, have no such luxury. For them, the union of man and woman, the man for the woman and the woman for the man, is crucial to the harmony and the success of daily life. Under those circumstances, everyone works hard, and the needs (and the beauties) of life are too immediate for sensible people to scrutinize which side of the scales drops the lower—whether the woman cleaning and cooking is working harder than the man plowing and harrowing.

The very division of labor, made necessary by the facts of life, taking best advantage of the man's nature and body and the woman's nature and body, makes man and woman dependent upon one another, and thus gives ample reason for gratitude. Each then becomes a *gift for the other*; and the gift is inseparable from the difference in sexual being.

I must insist upon this. I do not use the word *gender*, except to refer to the grammatical category. I'm quite aware of the nonsensical idea that sex is one thing, referring only to a minor bit of plumbing in the nether regions, and gender another, referring to everything else about men and women, all of it supposedly "socially constructed" and arbitrary. Yes, I've heard it all my academic life, and the more we actually learn about biological maleness and femaleness, the more absurd this line becomes. Every cell of my body is marked as masculine. My adrenal system is different from my wife's—it is primed for sudden attack and just as sudden calm; an adrenal system for all-out fighting, followed or preceded by cold strategy. Hers is not that way; I doubt that anyone caring for small children ought to be that way. My heart-lung capacity at age fifty is that of a woman at her peak, at age twenty. I will possess more brute strength (by far) than my daughter until I am very old, or in the last stages of a terminal disease. My wife sees things I do not see; she makes connections with people I would not make; she has the touch.

We're not just different people. We are of different sexes. There's a good reason why no society has ever dreamed up the idea that women should dig long trenches and canals in order to drain land for mass agriculture, while the men cook and clean and take care of the babies. The reason is called starvation. It is also called sanity: no sane woman would have stood for it.

The very word *sex* derives from Latin *sexus*, denoting that which separates. It is a mark of our degeneracy that the ugly term "having sex" has come to mean the marital act, with the once delicate term "making love" similarly demoted. What man and woman do in the marriage bed is not "having" sex; the sex, that is the separation, they are provided with already. What they do is to unite, across the separation. Let's consider that for a moment. The possession of sexual organs means, in the first instance, that we are biologically, naturally *oriented toward the other*. If a small child falls into the bad habit of manipulating himself over and over for his own pleasure, we gently but firmly teach him not to do that. On some level we understand that it is wrong, because those were not meant for our own pleasure merely. They are meant for the other sex. They are meant, indeed, for the complete donation of oneself in love for the one who *is not like me*.

Someone here will object, "That's all well and good, but I do not see how the recognition of same-sex marriages will cause me to love my wife any less than I do!" The objection misses the point. Actually, it misses three points.

The first is that revolutions in culture—or, since we no longer actually possess a culture, in mass habits—very seldom work upon any one individual in such an immediate way. When no-fault divorce became the law of the land, very few people lined up at the courthouse to procure one. A happily married man and woman woke up the next day apparently as happy as when they went to bed the night before. Yet no-fault divorce wrought a real revolution in the "culture" of marriage in the United States, or was a powerful engine in the revolution that was ongoing. Otherwise we should have to believe that law and custom have no influence whatever upon the lives of human beings, which is an absurdity, almost a contradiction in terms. The very definition of a custom is that it has become customary, and law either reflects what is customary or guides people towards what is believed should become customary; otherwise why have law at all?

So the sexual revolution *has already* wrought a "culture" in which men and women do not love one another as deeply and as gratefully as they ought to, and this is true despite any particular couple's devotion. I believe that any honest and careful observer must come to this conclusion. Nine hundred years ago in southern France, a tradition of lyric love poetry began, sometimes bawdy and merry, often almost religious in tenor, to sing the praises of the poet's lady love. For all those nine hundred years, that is what men have done. Robert Burns sang that his love was like a red, red rose; and the Italian folk artist Ernesto De Curtis begged his beloved to come back to Sorrento; and one William Douglas vowed that for his bonnie Annie Laurie, he'd lay him down and dee; and Stephen Foster, aching for the woman who had left him, sang that he dreamed of Jeannie with the light brown hair.

This tradition is in its death rattle. Why should we have expected otherwise? When men and women are taught, first, to use other people as objects of sexual excitement, not as if they were animals but as if they were toys or robots, do we really expect that they should all at once see the beauty and the nobility of the other sex? Call it the punishment of contempt. If you treat with contempt something that in reality claims your honor and your love, the contempt you cast redounds upon your own proper head. You become someone contemptible. So now popular musicians do not sing lyrically about a woman's beauty or a man's courage. Instead they whine or grunt like animals in a sweltering pen. They have almost nothing kind to say to one another.

Which brings me to the second point. A particular John may love his wife Jane well enough, but he cannot on his own supply, as it were, a third dimension to his love, the dimension of universality. He can't say, "My love for Jane is an instance of man's love for woman," because he does not feel that men really do love women. Much of what he sees testifies to the reverse.

It is no longer a commonplace. He has not heard men singing the praises of women, or women singing the praises of men. He hears insults and bursts of frustration and recrimination; and these we have always had with us. But the praise, never; the gratitude for the other sex, never. So too he cannot see that his love for his wife is a special form of his appreciation for all women. The love he bears her is personal, and it is good and holy as far as it goes. But it does not go far enough. It does not leave the front door.

And so to the third point. The very assumption behind the campaign for same-sex pseudogamy is that men are not for women and women are not for men, and that our sexual powers are for ourselves alone, to do with as we please without regard to biological nature, to children, and to the common good. It is radically individualistic. Indeed, young people are now encouraged to craft their own "genders," though it is impossible for me to fathom what any "gender" can possibly be, other than a flitting phantasm of the imagination, once the plain and solid reality of sex is denied. In such an environment, no one learns, from earliest years, to find fulfillment in surrendering the self in the most radical way, to the *other who is fundamentally not like me*, for a good that far transcends the transient pleasures of the body. That environment is an acid bath for love. It cannot kill all of the love between men and women, but it will kill much of that love, and it must inevitably corrode or curdle or cramp most of the rest. Even people who keep themselves free, in their persons, of the sickness that plagues the world will be cramped by that sickness; their love will lack its deserved scope for public action and public recognition. In Chaucer's day, in the village of Dunmowe, a whole side of bacon would be given once a year to the married couple who lived with one another in sweetest concord. Nothing comparable could now be imagined. A private party is all that the long-married couple merits.

But we must unite the sexes—not just a John and Mary here and there, but men and women generally, for one another. Unless they unite, the culture cannot survive. The women split away to protect their persons and their relatively few children, and grow harried and cynical; the unattached males pass the dull hours in frivolity or destruction.

Fourth Argument

We Must Recover the Virtues of Modesty and Purity

T HERE'S a scene in Shakespeare's *The Tempest* that I am especially fond of, though it's nearly impossible for the modern reader to understand. That's not because the language is difficult. It isn't. It is because the modern reader is apt to watch the clock, a mechanical device without meaning, rather than to watch the sun, or the growth of children, or the slow flourishing of crops, or the rise and fall of nations. Just as his attitude towards his own body is reductive—the body is something that his real "self," whatever that may be, possesses, just as a carpenter has a hammer or a saw in his toolbox—so also is his attitude toward time. Time is not the moving image of eternity, or even the bittersweet dwelling place of creatures as strange as we are, who remember and perceive and anticipate, who build castles for the future and sacred memorials for the distant past. Time is a neutral span to be reckoned by extent no more. If we have a lot of it, we can get a lot done, and if we don't have much left, that's too bad for us.

That was not Shakespeare's view. One moment, the twinkling of an eye, can change a human life utterly, even raise it from the grave of wickedness and despair. Shakespeare is ever urging us to *be ready for the time*, because each moment is pregnant with possibilities beyond our determination, even beyond imagining. That does not mean that we "make the most" of time, as someone does who crams experiences into it as a glutton crams food down his maw. It means that we surrender ourselves to what every moment requires of us as moral beings. We neither attempt to forestall it nor do we linger in indecision. We do not "bustle" in the world, as the villain Richard III does, who ends with a cry of futility, "A horse, a horse, my kingdom for a horse!" Nor do we loll back and pluck the sensual fruits of the day, ignoring our duty, as does the hapless Richard II, who says, sententiously but rightly, "I wasted time, and now doth time waste me." We are to be *yare*, as the sailors in *The Tempest* are, ready on the instant to haul the sails down on their ropes or to turn the mizzen against the wind, to do all that men can do in the urgent time, obeying the Master whose signals are whistled above the fury of the storm, and the Boatswain who is the Master's delegate, relaying his orders.

This scene, though, isn't on the water. It's in the poor cell of Prospero. His daughter Miranda and the prince of Naples, Ferdinand, have fallen in love with one another and have pledged their troth, as Prospero has secretly been hoping. And now that Ferdinand has passed the trials of his virtue, his future father-in-law welcomes him openly. Yet, after he says that his daughter will "outstrip all praise / And make it halt behind her," he warns Ferdinand against outstripping the right time:

> *Then, as my gift, and thine own acquisition*
> *Worthily purchased, take my daughter. But*
> *If thou dost break her virgin knot before*
> *All sanctimonious ceremonies may*
> *With full and holy rite be ministered,*
> *No sweet aspersion shall the heavens let fall*

To make this contract grow: but barren hate,
Sour-eyed disdain, and discord, shall bestrew
The union of your bed with weeds so loathly,
That you shall hate it both: therefore, take heed,
As Hymen's lamps shall light you.

To embrace in mock-marriage is like sowing seeds in the snow, or like tearing unripe fruit from the tree, or like leaving a plot of land untended. It is to invite weeds into what should be a garden. It is to get the time all wrong.

Ferdinand understands this, and in his reply he too uses images of time—and with a manly passion that shows that purity is a warm and life-loving virtue indeed:

As I hope
For quiet days, fair issue, and long life,
With such love as 'tis now; the murkiest den,
The most opportune place, the strong'st suggestion
Our worser Genius can, shall never melt
Mine honor into lust, to take away
The edge of that day's celebration,
When I shall think [either] Phoebus' steeds are foundered,
Or night kept chained below.

No suggestions of evil, no conjunction of place or time that would allow him to get away with the sin, will be hot enough to melt the steel of his honor and turn it into weak, contemptible lust. Is that because Ferdinand does not desire Miranda? Hardly! To appreciate Miranda—whose name, coined by Shakespeare, means "she who is deserving of wonder"—is to know that her beauty is but the lovely setting for her more admirable virtue. Ferdinand longs with the keenness of a sword for that wedding day, and after the day the night. What will he be thinking of on that day? That the horses of the Sun's chariot must have foundered, or night must have been kept in chains below the horizon. "Fairly bespoke," says Prospero with a smile, as he was a young man once, too.

The young man's love for Miranda is in harmony with his longing to see that day and that night, a day of celebration before God and man, and a night of consummation, in the private haven of the marriage bed. It is not *casual*, as if, with a shrug, one might say, "There's nothing else to do tonight, so I might as well go to bed with whatever her name is." It is not anticlimactic, as it must be if the act has come before the vow that gives the act its meaning. It is not the heedless act of an animal, or the calculated act of a pleasure-seeker, or the sad and sometimes desperate act of a human being who is hoping against hope that the person in the bed will love him or her when the morning breaks. It does not involve the self-contradiction of doing the child-making thing while thrusting the possibility of a child out of the imagination as a horror; or accepting the possibility of a child, without having first provided the child the ordered world of a permanent vow—the home of married love that every child needs and deserves.

To put the matter bluntly, no sense at all can be made of the virtue of purity if sodomy is countenanced or even celebrated. That is because the virtue is founded in reality, and the vice depends upon denying the reality. I don't mean that homosexuals are responsible for the decay of our sense of the virtue. I mean instead that our acceptance of sodomy is diagnostic—it shows how far we have already diverged from reality. The opium addict may have begun as an ordinary fellow going on binges of gin and tonic. He cannot return to health, now, by giving up just one activity; he has to give up both. He cannot be both sober and addicted to opium. Or, to move to the realm of motives, he cannot say, "It is wrong to abuse the body by hard liquor, because it compromises the health, it encourages sloth and irresponsibility, it clouds the mind and it sows anger and disappointment where love should reign," and then say, "But we will use opium instead." That makes no sense.

But my analogy is still not adequate to describe the absurdity. That is because alcohol may be used well—the wine that gladdens the heart, that makes for relaxation and conviviality. When a boy and girl fornicate, they are doing something of a kind that is more seriously wrong than are sins of intemperance. They are doing something natural, but in a way that cannot be right, in any degree. You can drink a little, but you can't fornicate a little. Even at that, they are doing what might have been not only permissible but cause for joy, if done within the bonds of matrimony. But that cannot apply to sodomy. There is no biological reason for sodomy. The body does not need it; society does not need it; in this sense it is not a sin involving the intemperate use of something good or morally neutral, nor is it a sin involving the misuse of such things. It is an act which by its nature frustrates the function of the organs of the body it employs.

In short, you cannot say to John and Mary, "You two must wait till marriage," while saying to Alan and Steve, "You two can go right ahead." What can chastity or purity even mean, once you have smiled at sodomy?

The question then arises, "Why should we care? What difference can it make if people practice or strive for or in any way honor the virtue of purity? Is it even a virtue at all? Isn't it the vice of repression?" That's what propagandists for the sexual revolution have long argued, and it's what proponents of the homosexual agenda take for granted. They see themselves as liberating people from the bonds of a supposed fear of sexual expression. Hence the "gay pride" parades, featuring people in aggressive states of undress, mimicking sex acts in public, and raucously flouting anything that's left of the sense of decency, which itself is but the shadow of the full-blooded virtue I am discussing.

First let's answer the charge of repression. It's a term we've held over from Freud, who, thinking in the mechanical terms of the industrial revolution, viewed the human mind as a machine rather like a boiler. If you "repress" the steam in a boiler and don't give it a safety valve, the boiler will blow a gasket or explode. The safety valve in question here is sexual release, which has to be allowed, if the human boiler is to remain healthy.

There are all kinds of problems with this way of thinking. Freud himself did not believe it. He saw that "repression"—to grant him the notion for the sake of argument—was necessary for civilization to develop. Change the arena from sexual expression to the expression of wrath. Imagine a society in which the delights of wrath are indulged, a society that is never more than a swing of an ax or a public insult away from a blood feud. No civilization can be built upon it. This is not simply a flight of my imagination. Aeschylus' trilogy, the *Oresteia*, has as its central problem exactly that, the ordering of the dark forces of wrath and vengeance—not their banishment, because in themselves and in their proper place they are good and to be revered—so that a free city may emerge, wherein reason and persuasion take the place of violence. It is not a matter of repression, but of transformation.

Orestes, the noble young son of Agamemnon, has secretly returned to Argos from exile. He has grown into the strength and the responsibilities of a man. He knows that he must avenge his father's death; the god Apollo himself has been spurring him on to do it. So has his sister Electra, who is moved by a girl's love for her father, but even more by an implacable hatred for her mother, Clytemnestra. For Clytemnestra is the murderess; she tangled Agamemnon in a net on the day when he returned to Argos from Troy, and slew him at his own altar, exulting in her act of vengeance—the house of Argos has been plagued by a long series of wicked deeds and wicked acts of vengeance against them. Orestes kills her, but wavers in the doing, and afterwards he is pursued by the Furies, hideous underworld goddesses of blood and madness, hounding him with guilt.

The quandary is resolved in the final play, *The Eumenides*, whose name itself is most revealing: The Kindly Ones. The scene is a trial on the rocky citadel of Athens. The goddess Athena presides, representing the ordered liberty of Aeschylus' beloved city. Apollo pleads for the defendant Orestes, while the Furies, the prosecutors, plead for their prescriptive right to avenge blood shed by a blood relation. We might expect from a very good playwright that Apollo would be given the better of the argument. He is, after all, one of the "younger" generation of gods, those sky-deities of light and laughter and beauty, who dwell with Zeus upon Mount Olympus. The Furies, meanwhile, are hideous, slavering, shrieking monsters, associated with the womb and the tomb, the dark world beneath our feet and within the pulses of our blood.

But Aeschylus is not just a very good playwright. He is, with Shakespeare and Sophocles, one of the three greatest playwrights who have ever lived. He surprises us by representing the Furies sympathetically, giving them at several points the better of the argument against Apollo. The trial seems to reach an impasse—how can we adjudge the guilt of a man caught between two evils, damned if he does and damned if he doesn't? The key figure is Athena. Unlike Apollo, she treats the Furies with respect, so that when she asks them if they would allow her to decide the case, they defer to her judgment. Athena then turns the matter over to the jurymen of Athens—that is, to men who have come together to listen to reasons and to decide what course to take for the common good. The jurymen split evenly, whereupon Athena casts the deciding vote, for acquittal.

When the Furies shriek in dismay, Athena soothes them by promising them a place of honor in that same citadel; she says that the Athenians will always pay them homage and pray for their favor. At this point they cease to be the Furies: they are now the Kindly Ones, who bless childbirth and the growth of crops and the city itself.

I beg the reader's pardon for what may seem a long digression. There's an analogy to draw between the use of the irascible drive and the use of the appetitive drive; between the relish for fighting and the relish for sexual consummation. Campaigns for mere abstinence fail because they miss the full human reality of sex, and so they shoot too low. The practice of abstinence is a negative merely. Such campaigns, well-meant though they are, hold up no ideal to strive for, nothing beautiful to honor. They do not guide the young in the right and full and lively use of that natural longing for love. It's like telling a young man, "You must suppress the anger you naturally feel when you are faced with injustice against the weak and the poor. You must pretend that you do not see the injustice. You may see a grown man attacking a woman or a child, and you will look the other way. You'll not clench your fists. You'll not throw a punch."

The virtue of fortitude requires the right use of anger. A man who rails left and right, swinging his fists whenever he perceives the slightest wrong, is not fit for civil life. A man who indulges his lust for fighting for the sheer animal thrill of it is not only uncivilized, he is beastlike. The man who shies away from the fight—the prude in matters of wrath—can live in a city, but such as he can never really build the city. That requires men whose capacity for anger is rightly ordered, as to the place and time and manner and degree of its action. Such men will be "angrier," so to speak, or more effective in their anger, than are men who simply dissipate their force in foolish and unnecessary fighting, or who become so inured to fighting that after a while they grow oppressed by boredom, and must, to capture the old thrill, swerve into that perversion of wrath's action which is cruelty.

Abstinence is to purity as nonviolence is to fortitude. The pure man or woman is not merely refraining from something that would give pleasure, as a dieter refuses the scoop of ice cream. The pure person has a clear and vibrant vision of the goodness of being male and being female. That is an occasion for reverence. It is entirely justified. "I am the sort of being that can beget a child," says the man, and "I am the sort of being that can bear a child," says the woman. And each, beholding the other, sees the goodness of his sex in relation to the goodness of the other. To see the goodness of being male is to see the goodness of being female, and vice versa, since the man is so obviously for the woman and the woman so obviously for the man.

So "repression" does not enter into the matter. Virtue does—and that brings me to the second point, implicit in the words we use to describe sexual vice, or the person who succumbs to it.

The word purity suggests something full of light and innocence, free of the encumbrances of baseness, lies, ignorance of true worth, and scorn. Imagine the embodiment of purity. She is Shakespeare's Rosalind in *As You Like It*, as far from a delicate hothouse flower as it is possible to be. She is sprightly, she meets adversity with courage, she has a sharp wit, and she is filled with a lively and youthful passion. She is, in all the flower of her powerful personality, wholly clean of heart. When she falls in love with Orlando, it isn't just that he's a strong and handsome young man—those are as common as acorns. It's that his loyalty to the memory of his father reflects her loyalty to her father who has been unjustly cast into exile; and his loneliness strikes a sympathetic chord in her heart. She and her dear cousin Celia try to persuade him not to risk his life in the wrestling match he has entered. He replies, abashed:

I beseech you, punish me not with your hard thoughts:
wherein I confess me much guilty, to deny so fair and
excellent ladies anything. But let your fair eyes and gentle
wishes go with me to my trial: wherein if I be foiled, there
is but one shamed that was never gracious; if killed, but
one dead that is willing to be so. I shall do my friends no
wrong, for I have none to lament me; the world no injury,
for in it I have nothing; only in the world I fill up a place,
which may be better supplied when I have made it empty.

This is not calculated. It is not even flirting. It comes straight from the clean heart of a good man. He has no stratagems. He engages in no subterfuge. When he praises the excellence of Rosalind and Celia, it is no rhetorical flourish. *He sees the excellence they do indeed possess*—and that excellence is inextricable from their womanly virtue. Rosalind falls in love on the moment—a love that is as far above the pettiness of lust as the bright star in the sky is above its reflection in the water of a ditch. "The little strength I have," she says, "I would it were with you."

And the lad surprises the court with a victory! When Rosalind congratulates him, he stands like a senseless stock. He isn't a smooth talker, and we appreciate him all the more for that. It's because the pure and good Rosalind *should* strike a young man speechless. But she assists him in his travail. "Sir," she says to him, "you have wrestled well, and overthrown / More than your enemies."

That's as much as to say, "I am yours forever." Of course, by the time young Orlando has understood what she's said, Rosalind has left the stage, though we know they are destined for one another in marriage. Now the whole force of this scene depends upon the cleanness of heart of the two young people falling in love. Yes, there's the natural attraction of beauty, but it is not animalized—as in our magazines, which reduce the human figure to flesh such as a canny butcher would divide into steaks. It is humanized, and that means that it is raised at least to the realm of moral virtue. If the actor and actress were to mug the scene by heavy breathing or other nonsense, they would rob the play of its wonder, and it would degenerate into a mildly prurient exercise in preparation for the bed. It would *sully* the principal characters and the comedy itself.

We sense that the human body is a precious thing, worthy of our reverence. It is not a tool, not an object of consumption like a steak or a keg of beer, not an animate provider of pleasure. It is the outward expression of a profound mystery, that of another human being. When we meet another person, when we look at his or her face, we are in the presence of a creature whose like we have never found in all the rest of the universe. The human person is open to infinity. He can do more than apprehend all the creatures he observes. He can imagine worlds he has never seen. And the human person comes to us embodied in two markedly different sexes. We never meet a human being merely: we meet men and women, boys and girls. What we believe about the honor and reverence that is due to that astounding mystery, the human person, we must believe also about being-male and being-female. It is a contradiction to say, "I honor the human person," while treating the human body as separable from the person, using it as a tool, devouring images of it, rubbing against it as a horse rubs his behind against a post.

So we mustn't say, "Despite his love for Rosalind, Orlando will not attempt to bring her to bed before the wedding day." That makes no sense. Really to love Rosalind or any person of such purity is to see the splendor of her virtue. One cannot at once love the beautiful and desire to defile it. One cannot love the *Pieta* with an ax. Because Orlando loves Rosalind truly, he will give himself completely to her and take her completely to him in body and in spirit together, in that land of marriage before man and God. Anything less would be a disillusioning lie.

When we treat with contempt something that shines and claims our reverence, we cast dirt upon it—all human languages are at one in this insight. The old word for pornography was smut, meaning filth; not good, rich, black soil, but moral squalor, defiling those who make it and those who consume it. With smut, we begin by taking a perverse delight in the forbidden, despite the filth. Then the filth itself exercises its fascination, and we seek not a wrong use of something good, but the dabbling in something wicked and bizarre. After a while, even the filth is hardly noticeable anymore, just as someone who lives in a pigsty or a sewer can no longer smell the stench.

If this were a plague rotting the souls of individual men and women here and there, it would be bad enough, and in charity towards our weaker brothers and sisters we should act to cordon off the extent of the disease, seeking to limit its extent and its vigor as far as is possible in a free and well-ordered polity. But indulgence in filth isn't like that. It does not confine itself to the individual. Therefore the virtue of purity must matter to everyone—it helps to determine what kind of society we will have. And it was precisely to fashion a wholly new society, and not to promote individual liberty, that "free love" and licentiousness were first promoted.

If I pour raw sewage and garbage into the ditch in front of my house, I'm not forcing you to touch it or to soil your meals with it; but I am forcing you to live in its neighborhood. You must endure the smell. You must endure the rats and skunks and raccoons that will be attracted to it. If my example catches on, if even one in ten homeowners does the same, you will live in a nausea-making place, regardless of your own decisions.

If anything, my analogy here is still too weak to express the extent of the harm done. That's because no personal relations are involved in the pollution of the ditch in front of a house. But the customs and the moral laws governing the relations between the sexes constitute a language we all must use. I'll be examining this matter more closely in a later chapter. You may own a private open cesspool. You cannot speak a private language. A moral cesspool can never really be private, for the simple reason that good and evil in human life involve us all together; we are in one moral boat, we drink the same water of moral instruction; we breathe the same cultural air.

Sins against purity are performed (at least we hope so) in private, but the effect is public and involves us all. We see this in the so-called "hookup culture" on college campuses. A male and a female—I can't grace them with the innocent names of boy and girl, or the honorable names of man and woman—use one another as un-persons, casually, for sexual release. Far from intending a lifelong love but in the wrong way, they do not intend love at all. The agents pretend that the arrangement is strictly temporary. Of course, one or another of them may secretly harbor a desire that it would last forever, but that desire—that deeply human, normal, commendable desire, here expressed in a foolish and absurd and immoral way—must skulk in the shadows. *That* now becomes the love that dare not speak its name—ordinary human love.

In a land riddled by bribe-taking politicians and protection rackets and dirty dealing, the man who attempts to preserve his honesty will be *immiserated:* he will be compelled to do business in a context in which all the right decisions will hurt him in the short run, and in the long run may destroy him. He is denied the cultural support that he deserves. He is denied, if you will, healthy air to breathe and clean water to drink. He must adapt to the evil game, compromising his integrity and therefore his very humanity, or cower in a corner, like a plant that barely manages to eke out a scraggly life under bad conditions, or die.

And that is what faces the young person who has a strong sense of the integrity of being-male and being-female, who sees the true beauty of sex in the fullness of its child-making potential, in its radical openness to generations past and to come, and in its brave self-surrender to the *other*.

That person is immediately immiserated. He is robbed of his right to flourish in a truly human culture. No one is perfect, and no culture is perfect—far from it. But all healthy cultures reward virtue and punish vice, encourage what is noble and beautiful and discourage what is base and tawdry, promote liberty and restrain license. He now must dwell in a perverse anti-culture in which his attempt to practice the demanding virtue of purity meets less than approval. It meets snorts of disdain and ridicule. In a healthy culture, he would not be alone, and it would not be hard for him to meet a young lady of similar mind. Married men and women, in a healthy culture, would take upon themselves the cheerful task of bringing such boys and girls together, in those innocent and lively pastimes that are the seedbed of sexual attraction and love; in dances and concerts and parties attended by everyone from toddlers to grandparents hobbling on their canes.

Instead, they fall, not to passion, to which all people are subject and against which the strongest of us is feeble enough, but to loneliness, boredom, cynicism, and heedlessness. Passion wrongly directed is a human thing and the stuff of tragedy. Ask Mark Antony, who for his adulterous love of Cleopatra gave up his chance to rule the world. Ask Canio, that laughing and weeping hero of *I Pagliacci*, who stabs his wife and her lover on stage during their performance of a play, and then says to the audience, "The comedy is over." But the world of the hookup, the world fashioned by a complete rejection of the virtue of purity and its insights into manhood and womanhood, that world does not rise to the level of tragedy. Its very filth is antiseptic;

it is not clean, but blank and empty. When the male-thing and the female-thing remove their clothes but not their selfishness, when they take from the other while promising nothing, when they urge their bodies to mimic a passion which they not only do not feel but which they are taught they *should not feel*, lest it complicate their passage toward wealth and prestige, they are less than human and other than beasts. They are beyond loneliness.

But others, those in the far greater number, who have not raised that inches-thick callus upon the soul, they are not beyond loneliness. Some of them, like the would-be honest men in the anticulture of deceit, do what they know they should not do, shaming themselves, but seeking for purity as it were in a brothel; seeking for love in a land bristling with egotism, treachery, ambition, cold hedonism, and indifference. They capitulate. They agree to go to bed with someone, on the off chance that love will eventually come round; perhaps, she says to herself, when he wakes up he will still want to look at me. Perhaps, he says, when she wakes up she will remember my name. Others do not shame themselves, and so it happens that the very men and women who in a sane world would be most admired and most obviously successful in marriage remain alone, one here and one there.

The sexual revolution is essentially a lonely one. That's not just a matter of the results. Loneliness is its brick and mortar. For the sexual revolution isolates. The man says to himself, "I will have this woman now, because it is convenient, but I'll make sure she doesn't press things further." The woman says to herself, "I'll let this man have his way, because he's weak and I can manipulate him for my pleasure." Each one says, "We must make sure that no third person intrudes upon this arrangement," the third person that is the natural, biological result of what should be married love but which instead is idle lust. If that third person does so intrude, he may well be dispatched, with cold steel and antisepsis. His remains will be deposited in a bag labeled "biohazard." A human life—a biohazard—actually only a hazard to the false lives of those who engage in false love, subordinated to a false sense of progress or achievement. As I've said, most people have not so radically eviscerated themselves of their humanity. Most people, in the secret chambers of their hearts, would well wish to live in a different world, one in which purity was honored. Most people still feel the loss. They know that it is a better thing to be Rosalind than to be the sluttish "star" whose sexual escapades are blared across the headlines of magazines in drug stores. They know that it is a better thing to be Orlando than to be the cad who treats women with less honor to their womanhood than he would grant to the doghood of his retriever.

They see a world that is vile at every turn—one in which, even before puberty, most children will have pored over things which people of past generations not only had not seen but could not have imagined, for their squalor and perversity; a horrible world in which children are owl-eyed and precocious and adults are childish and selfish. That is the world of the sexual revolution. They see it, these sad compromisers, and feel powerless to do anything about it. So the corruption spreads.

And much of the sweetness of human youth dies. How so? It's characteristic of our loss of a genuine culture that we tend to forget about the great, important *middle ground* where we live most of our lives. We remember the individual, which really is an abstraction or a truncation of full human life and action, and we remember the State, which is another kind of abstraction, the farther it is removed from the lives of ordinary human beings where they live and work and play and learn and worship. We forget all the middle institutions where culture thrives and where human beings have their most fruitful fields of action. We forget the local school, locally directed, and the neighborhood, with its own traditions and its form of self-policing, and the family, that natural society, with rights and duties that precede the existence of any state.

The same amnesia afflicts us in our arguments about sexual morality. We have forgotten the whole country between abstinence and marriage. We have forgotten, in other words, that in a culture that honors purity, boys and girls will enjoy the freedom and the leisure to learn what the other sex is about. A kiss may be just a kiss, and a sigh just a sigh. I have seen a book published as late as 1965, for young Catholics, whose main chapters on sex were devoted not to the evils of perversion, to venereal diseases that now number about thirty, to snuffing out human life, and to pornography. No, they were devoted to the feeling of falling in love, to "going steady," and to kissing.

Boys now in high school and college do not ask girls out for dates. They can't. There is no "language" for them to use, no common understanding of what a word or an action is to mean. If he says, "I'd like to take you to a movie," what does that imply? In a more innocent time, it meant that he'd take the girl to a movie, and he might be brave enough to put an arm around her shoulder, or even to steal a kiss. In a more innocent time, the kiss itself would be a delight. To walk home with the girl he likes best, holding her hand, would thrill him to the core of his being. A blushing kiss at the front door might have been the stuff of dreams; sweeter by far than anything that the bored addict can glean from a hundred pages of body parts.

The bad language has driven out the good. So the boy who knows he should not be play-acting at marriage with a girl now dare not kiss her with any passion or hold her hand or give her a warm embrace. All those actions now have lost their old meanings, and have become mere preludes to sexual congress. Therefore we hardly ever see them. Boys do not give girls flowers or write poems for them. They do not court them. Girls do not present themselves to be courted. If they tease boys, it isn't innocent flirtation. A movement that was supposed to bring people together in some grand summer of love has wrought mass alienation. The evidence is there for all to see, or rather not to see, but to miss, as I do not see boys and girls flirting in a childlike way, or kissing, or holding hands, or bowling at the alley, or dressing up for one another, or giving valentines to one another. At Yale, Valentine's Day is "celebrated" by Sex Week, complete with the sale of sex toys and how-to presentations by prostitutes. At many colleges, it is "celebrated" by the angry feminist twaddle, *The Vagina Monologues*, in which spoiled and corrupted college women cry out their independence from predatory males by shouting the vulgar name for their private parts. Anger, resentment, self-promotion, immodesty, cruelty, callousness, perversion; try now asking that girl over there what her name is and whether she'd go with you to the ice cream social.

Again I insist upon the point. The whole of the sexual revolution has been a colossal failure, and has wrought untold human misery. The move for same-sex pseudogamy is inextricable from that revolution; it is grafted upon it and cannot survive or even appear to make sense without it. We cannot have a good nation unless we are a good people. We cannot be a good people when we throw contempt upon manhood and womanhood and the virtue that honors their beauty and their being for one another; it is like asking for clean sleaze, or cold love.

Fifth Argument

*We Should Not Foreclose the Opportunity
for Members of the Same Sex to Forge
Friendships with One Another That Are
Chaste, Deep, and Physically Expressed*

SAM Gamgee has been fool enough to follow his beloved
master Frodo into Mordor, the realm of death. To rescue
Frodo from the orcs who have taken him captive and who will
slay him as soon as he ceases to be of use in finding the Ring,
Sam has fought the monstrous spider Shelob, has eluded the
pursuit of the orcs, and has dispatched a few of them to their
merited deaths. Finally he finds Frodo in the upper room of a
small, filthy cell, naked, half-conscious, lying in a heap in a corner. "Frodo! Mr. Frodo, my dear!" he cries. "It's Sam, I've come!"
With a bluff tenderness he clasps him to his breast, assuring
him that it is really he, Sam, in the flesh.

Still groggy, Frodo can hardly believe it, but he clutches at
his friend. It seems to him all the tissue of a dream—that an
orc with a whip has turned into Sam—and it is all mixed up
with the sound of singing that he thought he heard and tried
to answer. "That was me singing," says Sam, shaking his head

and saying that he had all but given up hope of ever finding his friend again. He cradles Frodo's head, as one would comfort a troubled child.

At that a snigger rises from the audience in the theater. *"What, are they gay?"*

It's an ignorant but inevitable response. In fact, it is the response that our students are fairly compelled to make. They *must be taught to see* homosexuality everywhere, to break down their natural tentativeness to accept the unnatural. So everyone who can no longer testify in his own defense must be dragooned. Shakespeare, or his narrative persona, expressed in his sonnets a passionate love for an unnamed and not too loyal young man, so Shakespeare must have been homosexual. All of our students "know" this, and have to know it, have to have their minds battered with it, despite the absence of any shred of biographical evidence, and despite the persona's explicit statement in sonnet 20 that the young man's sexual accoutrements are of no interest (or use) to him whatever.

The bachelor Abe Lincoln long shared a bed with his closest friend, Joshua Speed, and later wrote letters expressing, with what seems a touch of self-deprecating irony, his fear that he would be lonely once Speed had taken a wife. Lincoln therefore must be homosexual. Or, if not that, then what we have here is "homosocial," a tricky term invented to suggest a likeness where none exists; as if football players, sailors, comrades in the infantry, and Shriners were somehow secretly gay, and so secretly indeed that it remained a secret to themselves and their wives and children and friends and everybody else too. No matter that men (and women too) commonly shared beds, and also commonly spoke of their friendship in strong, earthy language that now embarrasses. The poet Spenser used to share a bed with his friend and fellow scholar at Cambridge, Gabriel Harvey. There you go.

"Your love to me was finer than the love of women," laments David in a public song, when he learns of the death of his friend Jonathan. We know why. The godlike hero Gilgamesh and his friend Enkidu walk hand in hand into the dark forest of Humbaba. No wonder then that at Enkidu's death Gilgamesh will weep inconsolably, letting his hair grow long, flinging away his royal robes, and leaving the city to wander in the wilderness. Robert Falcon Scott enjoyed friendships so powerful, they moved men to venture with him into the Antarctic; and there they suffered with him the last terrible storm, only a few miles away from camp and survival; and there they died.

How have we come to this pass? The corrupted language has driven out the natural. We no longer have words to describe these friendships—or even to conceive of them. Except among certain well-protected groups, in most unusual circumstances, the reality itself must disappear, and the "friendship" of man and man or woman and woman must wither and fade into a wraith of its former self.

"That can't be!" you say. "What has language to do with my feelings for my friends?" Well, language is what we use to organize our perceptions of things. That is why totalitarians have always set about to control language. George Orwell makes the principle quite clear in his novel *Nineteen-Eighty Four*. The linguist Syme, employed by the Ministry of Truth, attempts to persuade the protagonist Winston Smith that "Newspeak," the dumbed-down language of the party's newspapers, is really quite a beautiful thing, precisely because it is not beautiful at all. Its power and wisdom lie in its incapacity to express any subtle thought. "Why have all those adjectives," says Syme, "like *excellent* and *superb* and *fine*, when simply *good* will do, or, for emphasis, *plusgood*, or *doubleplusgood*?" Foolish people think that the "reform" of language is intended to make it more efficient. Syme knows better. He tells Smith that it is to make heresy against the State—*thoughtcrime*—quite impossible, because men will no longer have the verbal capacity to think it. Smith listens with appalled fascination, and considers that Syme knows too much for his own good, and will probably not be long for the world. Smith's guess turns out to be correct.

If you have the power—if you are the editor of a series of textbooks to be read by millions of young people—you can so constrict the language or so distort it as to ensure that *thought-crime* does not occur. You can, for instance, make sure that pictures of soldiers are female, and pictures of hair stylists are male. You can studiously avoid the words "mother" and "father." You can avoid all reference to such virtues as womanliness and manliness. You can excise all stories of masculine honor and camaraderie. You can excise all stories of feminine gentleness and their care for children. You want them not to have the very tools they need to form the idea of a virtuous man or a virtuous woman. You couch everything in an unnatural language, such as Newspeak.

It's a strange double life you lead, if you are someone like Syme. You profess fascination with language, yet you abandon any deep study of it, and you certainly don't believe that it will reveal things that are everlastingly true about mankind. You don't submit to be instructed by it, just as you don't submit to be instructed by all the folk wisdom of fables and fairy tales and proverbs. Instead you are suspicious of all such things, because they are close to nature, and it is nature you want to subvert or supplant. You do not allow language to flourish within your soul, or within the souls of your students. Instead you turn it into a tool for dismantling the idea of natural order, and for establishing your own order in its place and imposing it on everyone else. The language war of the early feminists, a war they have won resoundingly, despite the occasional embarrass-ing rout (anyone remember "waitron"?), was about ushering in a new order, or rather a new and unnatural disorder. They were wrong who thought it was only a silly argument over words.

We can no more, each of us, fabricate our own opinions and customs concerning the sexes, than we can invent and speak our own private language. The sexual revolutionists—they who profess that what two consenting adults do with their privates in private is nobody's business—understand that the language had to be changed to assist the realization of their dream, and also that the realization of their dream would change the world, because it would change the language for everyone else. Language is not language if it is not communal; it is a neat trick of political abracadabra to argue for an individual's right to change the very medium of our thought and our social intercourse. If clothing is optional on a beach, then that is a nude beach. It cannot be a nude beach for some and an ordinary beach for others. To wear clothes at that beach at the very least means something that it had not meant before. If you may paint your house phosphorescent orange and violet, and you persuade a couple of your neighbors to do likewise, you no longer have what anybody would call a historic neighborhood.

If all of Kate's friends leap into bed with whatever male gives them a hearty dinner at Burger King and a round of miniature golf, and Kate chooses instead to kiss her date once on the cheek and leave him on the porch, she will suggest to everybody that she is a prude. She may be, or may not be; she may be more firmly in the grip of lust than they are, for all we know, and may just detest the boy. But her actions have connotations they did not use to have.

Imagine a world wherein the taboo has been broken and incest is loudly and defiantly celebrated. Your wife's unmarried brother puts his hand on your daughter's shoulder. That gesture, once innocent, must now mean something, or at least suggest something. If the uncle were wise and considerate, he would not make it in the first place. You see a father hugging his teenage daughter as she leaves the car to go to school. The possibility flashes before your mind. The language has changed, and the individual can do nothing about it.

By now the reader must see the point. Open homosexuality, loudly and defiantly celebrated, changes the language for everyone. If a man throws his arm around another man's waist, it is now a sign, whether he is on the political right or the left, whether he believes in biblical proscriptions of homosexuality or not. One of my students told me that he was at a bar with his best friend, and the fellow was weeping freely because his fiancée had broken up with him. In came a girl, chirping, "Oh, are the two of you gay?" Nobody would have assumed that when my father was a boy. Nobody would have assumed it even when I was a boy. I've seen an advertisement in a ladies' magazine from sixty years ago, for a four-head shower stand, so that four kids could shower underneath it at once. The ad featured a cartoon of four kids doing just that, after a ballgame. That ad could not now be produced; actually, the shower head itself could not be produced, because the matter-of-factness no longer holds. If you're walking in the woods and you come upon a pond where two teenage kids are skinny-dipping, the first thing you will think about is that they are not just friends, and you will think it despite the obvious fact that until swim trunks were invented this was exactly how two men or boys would go for a swim.

Because language is communal, the individual can choose to make a sign or not. He cannot determine what the sign is to mean, not to others, not to the one he signals, and not even to himself.

Friendship and the signs upon which it must subsist are in a bad way. I'll focus on the friendships of men, since that is what I know about; many comparable things might be said about the friendships of women, who have told me that they are beginning to feel the same constriction. We still have the word "friendship," and we still have something of the reality, but it is distant, dilute, bloodless. For modern American men, friendship is no longer forged in the heat of battle, or in the dust of the plains as they drive their herds across half a continent, or in the choking air of a coalmine, or even in the cigar smoke of a debating club. That is partly because our lives, for better and for worse, no longer involve the risk and the sweat that was the cement of deep friendship. No man will help hew the oaks for our cabin, because we no longer live in cabins. No man will stand by as we jump overboard to set the trawling net, because we have no boat and set no net; we live too comfortably for that. Under such fortunate circumstances, we need all the more the camaraderie and intellectual risk of the club.

But gentlemen's clubs have vanished or have been sued out of existence. (The Citadel, which had been one of the last three or four all-male schools in the country, is not The Citadel anymore, as the woman lawyer who sued it to death herself admitted, unwittingly and with amazing intellectual amnesia; on Monday arguing that her female client wanted the same experience the young men then enjoyed, and after her victory on Tuesday crowing that a student's experience at the Citadel would now be forever changed.) More than ever do men need to come together to eat and drink and argue and think, because more than ever their work separates them from each other; but now they are virtually forbidden to do so.

It's more of the devastation wrought by the sexual revolution. That we fail to see it as such is no surprise. Naturally, when we think of that recrudescence of paganism, we think of the bad things in front of us that we can see, and not of the good things that are missing, whose very absence makes it hard for us to call them to mind. We think first of its damage to the family and to relations between men and women. We think of divorce, pornography, unwed motherhood, abortion, and birthrates that in many nations in the West have fallen so low as to constitute a slow suicide. But the sexual revolution has also nearly killed male friendship as devoted to anything beyond drinking and watching sports; and the homosexual movement, a logically inevitable result of forty years of heterosexual promiscuity and feminist folly, bids fair to finish it off and nail the coffin shut.

And who will suffer the worst for it? Precisely those whom our society, stupidly considering them little more than pests or dolts, has ignored. I mean boys.

How so? Return to the example of Lincoln. His age was surely not more tolerant of homosexuality or of sexual deviancy than is ours. Accounts of the Civil War show young men brought to the brink of despair by their inability to break the habit of self-abuse. How, then, if deviancy was such a reproach, could Lincoln risk sharing a bed with a man and having the fact be publicly known? But that's the point. Only in such a case is the bed-sharing possible.

I'm sorry to have to use strong language, but only when sodomy is treated as a matter of course for everyone (as in the institutionalized buggery of boys and young men in ancient Sparta), or when it is met with such opprobrium that nobody would assume that a good man would engage in it, could the bed be shared. The stigma against sodomy cleared away ample space for an emotionally powerful friendship that did not involve sexual intercourse, exactly as the stigma against incest allows for the physical and emotional freedom of a family. In Japan, families bathe together, and it is considered a mark of the highest honor and the deepest trust to be invited, as an outsider, to join them. This custom is only made possible by the assumption that any sexual dalliance among family members, including anyone invited to "belong" to the family, is absolutely out of the question.

The converse is also true. If your society depends upon such emotionally powerful friendships—if the fellow feeling of comrades in arms is necessary for your survival—then you can protect the opportunity for such friendships in only two ways. You may go the strange route of Sparta, or you may demand on pain of expulsion from the group that such friendships will not be sexualized. Essentially you must do for all-male groups exactly what a husband and wife must do with regard to other members of the opposite sex. That doesn't mean that everyone will observe the restrictions. If we say we are without sin, the truth is not in us. But the public acknowledgment of standards of behavior creates the "language" which we will use and which will structure our relations. We have to use words that make sense, even though some people may use them to tell lies. Adulterers and sodomites there will be, but they must be called so, that we may have chaste spouses and bosom friends.

How does this latest twist of the sexual revolution hurt boys in particular? Some will say that it leaves them more vulnerable to be preyed upon by older men, and I have no doubt that this is true, given the psychological springs of male homosexuality, given the historical examples of ancient Greece and samurai Japan (among others), given the prominence of boy prostitutes at gay-friendly destinations, and given the terrible fact that many homosexual men were themselves abused as boys. That, by the way, should stop the mouths of people who claim that homosexual men were "born that way"—born to be molested? Absolutely determined to have a cruel or negligent father? Your father had to leave your mother, or had to die, when *you were six years old*, because something that he did or that happened to him *was in your DNA*?

But I don't want to overemphasize the vulnerability to abuse. Most homosexual men abide by the law. I mean something quite different.

The prominence of male homosexuality changes the language for teenage boys. It is absurd and cruel to say that the boy can ignore it. Even if he would, his classmates will not let him. All boys need to prove that they are not failures. They need to prove that they are on the way to becoming men: that they are not going to relapse into the need to be protected by, and therefore identified with, their mothers. Societies used to provide them with clear and public ways to do this. The Plains Indians would insert hooks into the flesh of their thirteen-year-old braves and hang them in the sun by those hooks, for hours. It was a test of endurance and courage. Those boys might well observe their older brothers, their fathers, and their uncles participating in the grueling ritual of the sun, whereby they would hook the flesh of their chests to bonds and attempt to burst free of the hooks by force, sometimes stretching their flesh like rubber, in ten foot long bands.

Too barbaric for us? What about observant Jews? At his bar-mitzvah the Jewish boy reads from the Holy Torah and announces, publicly, that on this day he has become a man. He has become, literally, a Son of the Commandment. In ancient Rome, a teenage boy would be given his first *toga virilis*, the garb of a man, and the family would have a big celebration in his honor. But in our carelessness we have taken such signs away from boys and left them to fend for themselves. Two choices remain. The boys must live without public recognition of their manhood and without their own certainty of it, or they must invent their own rituals and signs.

And here the sexual revolution comes to peddle more of its poison. The single incontrovertible sign of manhood that the boy can now seize on is that he has "done it" with a girl, and the earlier and more regularly and publicly he does it, the safer and surer he will feel. For proof, I call to witness the poorer classes in America, in derelict towns where all the industry has moved away, and in the welfare-ridden districts of our cities. If sex is easy to find, and if (as mothers of good-looking teenage boys will testify) the girls themselves seek it out, then you must have a pressing and publicly recognized excuse for not having sex. To avoid scandal, you must be protected by your being a linebacker on the football team, or by being too homely for any girl to be interested in you.

A boy who does not agree to a girl's demand for sex will be tagged with homosexuality. She will slander him herself. These are young people who, if you ask them, will boldly declare their support for the proposition that a man *can marry* a man; they have learned that lesson well. They lack any sensible language with which to think about sex and marriage. But that does not stop them from being naturally repulsed by the actual deeds. So we end up with the worst of two worlds. The bad behavior is condoned, *and it is suspected everywhere*, and made fun of, without mercy. There was an effeminate kid in my high school class, who was one of the most popular people around. Nobody assumed that he was homosexual, because we were in a Catholic school and, for various reasons, some of which had to do with the Faith, we tended to treat people a little more considerately than that. If he were in school now, everyone would assume that he was "gay," everybody would profess to believe that that was just fine, and he would be an object of constant, scornful, belittling, defensive, ridiculous chatter.

So the boy who does not want to be an object of this relentless attention will have to prevent it. Ask teenagers; they will tell you. Even a linebacker known as a rake will not dare to venture into the dangerous territory of too-close association with the wrong sort. He, too, will avoid the close male friendship. The popular and athletic boys will have their tickets punched, while other ordinary boys live under suspicion, alienated from the girls, and from one another.

This must happen. In large part, it has already happened. But we must try to remember when it was not so, if we are going to gauge what we have lost.

So far, I've lamented the attenuation of male friendships, which suffer under a terrible pincers attack. The libertinism of our day thrusts boys and girls together long before they are intellectually and emotionally ready for it. At the same time, the defiant promotion of homosexuality makes the natural and once powerful friendships among boys virtually impossible. Anyone can count up the resulting cases of venereal disease and teen pregnancies. A few social analysts of more penetrating insight can note what is unquantifiable, the despair among our young people, the dullness in the eye, the feeling that people are never to be trusted, that to fall in love is to be a contemptible fool. Yet the most daunting task of all is to mark the good things that this sexual precocity has smothered in the very birth. It is to note what should be there and is not. It is one thing to say that it has made friendships among boys more distant and difficult, and to suppose that that is a bad thing for the emotional lives of those boys. It is quite another, and it takes someone willing to see through our jaded dalliance with androgyny, to see that the loss of such friendships stunts the boys intellectually and goes a long way towards depriving everybody of the benefits that such intellectual development used to provide.

Consider how strong and audacious are the emotions of the young man. Suppose these are not directed towards sexual liaisons and playing house with young women. They do not therefore cease to exist; they must find some object. In the past that object would be the world and the male group's conquest of it.

The boys might get together to build a car from scratch. They might set up a series of telegraph connections. They might pitch themselves into learning everything they could about aircraft carriers and bombers. They might form a club to read Nietzsche, or to read the Scriptures, or to read both; audacity at this age can be wildly inconsistent. They might attach themselves to an acknowledged teacher, as did the young men of Athens who followed the chaste Socrates, or, dare I say, the young men of Palestine who followed Jesus. They might form guilds to ensure that the men they paid to teach them actually followed through on their end of the bargain; and thus would they create the medieval university. They might invent jazz music. They might rob banks.

They might do a thousand things fascinatingly creative and dangerously destructive, but one thing they would not do. They would not, as our boys do now, stagnate. They would be alive.

Edison formed such attachments. As early as age thirteen he had sought and found the men who could teach him all they knew about the telegraph. Louis Agassiz and his comrades defied death in mapping and studying glaciers. George Gershwin one day left one group of buddies playing stickball in the streets to go to the house of the boy who would be his lifelong friend and associate, Maxie Rosenzweig (later Max Rosen), from whom he learned the wonders of music. Lewis and Tolkien and their friends formed the Inklings and set their stamp on literary Christianity for a century.

Read the correspondence of Louis Pasteur, and you will come away thinking that the entire edifice of chemical research in France and Germany was built upon male friendship, the bonds of comrades going forth to battle. The language of these letters, to and from dozens of fellow scientists, is powerful and unashamedly personal. "I am touched by your acknowledgment of my deep and sincere affection for you," writes the elder chemist Jean-Jacque Biot to Pasteur,

and I thank you for it. But whilst keeping your attachment for me as I preserve mine for you, let me for the future rejoice in it in the secret recesses of my heart and of yours. The world is jealous of friendships however disinterested, and my affection for you is such that I wish people to feel that they honor themselves by appreciating you, rather than that they should know that you love me and that I love you.

What man has the space to feel anything comparable now, or the language to express it?

Our boys are failing in school. Has it occurred to no one that we have checked them at every turn, perversely insisting that they must not form brotherhoods, that they must not identify their manhood with practical and intellectual skills that transform the world, and that they must not ever have the opportunity, apart from girls, to attach themselves in friendship to men who could teach them? For good reason boys of that awkward age used to build tree houses and hang signs barring girls. They knew, if only instinctively, that the fire of the friendship could not subsist otherwise. But what similar thing can they do now without inviting either reproach or suspicion? Thus what is perfectly natural and healthy, indeed very much needed for certain people at certain times or for certain purposes, is cast as irrational and bigoted, or dubious and weak; and thus some boys will cobble together their own brotherhoods that eschew tenderness altogether, criminal brotherhoods that land them in prison. This is all right by us, it seems. Better to harass the Boy Scouts on Monday, and on Tuesday build another wing for the Ministry of Corrections.

And what about the emotional damage? We learn from researchers who are willing to be derided by the sexual politicians that one of the prompts for male homosexuality is precisely the disappointed desire, in certain boys, to form strong and physically expressed friendships with other boys. In our careless cruelty we have failed to protect all those whose feelings, as teenagers, are confused or ambiguous. If a teenage boy knows that nothing can happen between him and another boy, and if he knows that everybody else, including the other boy, knows it too, that knowledge must provide him the assurance that he can draw close to his friend.

He can "know" that it means only friendship, even if in another and fouler world it might mean more. He can rest easy with himself, because the meaning of his gestures and actions depends not on his confused and turbulent feelings, but upon an objective linguistic fact. Such a young man can thus negotiate his way through troubled times, fulfilling his need—and, if he has had a cruel father, it may be an aching need—for friendship, without corrupting his sexuality and without rejecting the possibility that he will become a true father and husband.

I do not know what agonies of loneliness and insecurity Abraham Lincoln, who did indeed have a cold father, suffered. But I assert that his lifeline for not becoming homosexual was the very same friendship that our revolutionists say was proof that he was. In the name of protecting homosexuals, we ignore the feelings of boys and snatch from them their dwindling opportunities to forge just such friendships whereof homosexual relations are a delusive mimicry.

On three great bonds of love do all cultures depend: the love between man and woman in marriage; the love between a mother and her child; and the camaraderie among men, a bond that used to be strong enough to move mountains. The first two have suffered greatly; the third has almost ceased to exist. Think about that friendship the next time you see the aging adolescents parading in feather boas or leather underpants as they march down Main Street, making their sexual proclivities known to everybody whether everybody cares or not. With every chanted slogan and every blaring sign, they crowd out the words of friendship and appropriate the healthy gestures of love between man and man. Confess: has it not left you uneasy even to read the words of that last sentence?

What do the paraders achieve, with their public promotion of homosexuality? They come out of the closet, and hustle a lot of good and natural feelings back in. They indulge in garrulity, and consequently tie the tongues and chill the hearts of men, who can no longer feel what they ought, or speak what they feel.

Reader, the next time you feel moved to pity the kindly and delicate man in the workstation near you, give a thought also to an adolescent somewhere, one among uncounted millions, a kid with acne maybe, a kid with an idea or a love, who needs a friend. Know then that your tolerance for the flambeau, which is little more than a self-congratulating cowardice, or your easy and poorly considered approval of the shy workmate's request that he be allowed to "marry" his partner, means that the unseen boy will not find that friend, and that the idea and the love will die.

No doubt about this. If you are a modern man, a half-man, many such ideas and loves have already died in you. For as much as you can admire them wistfully, from a half-understanding distance, you can be neither Frodo nor Sam, nor the man who created them. You dare not follow Agassiz, alone, to the Arctic. You will not weep for Jonathan. You once were acquainted with Enkidu, but that was all. Do not even mention John the Apostle.

Friendship, rest in peace.

Sixth Argument

We Must Not Condone All Forms of Consensual Activity among Adults

ALL of the great philosophers of the western tradition believed that virtue was liberating and vice enslaving, regardless of one's wealth or political status. Even the austere hedonist Epicurus believed it, which was why his follower, the Latin poet Lucretius, recommended not sexual adventures but the stability of marriage with an ordinary woman of acceptable looks and modest behavior. That isn't the full truth about marriage, not by a long shot, but it's saner than the chaos we have now. Liberty is one thing, and libertarianism as a doctrinaire project, ignoring the realities of our bodies and our flawed human nature and our common life, is another.

The question I'd like to ask here, then, is not what next thing we are going to approve if we approve of the pseudogamous unions of husband and husband, or wife and wife, but what things we have already in principle approved once we have approved of that, and whether those things conduce to human flourishing, the common good, and the liberty that flows from virtue.

No culture in history has accepted (let alone celebrated) homosexual acts between adult men or adult women, not even the ancient Greeks. In the Athens of Socrates and Plato, homosexual activity was almost exclusively what we would call pedophilic. It wasn't universally accepted, either. In Plato's *Symposium*, the homosexual Pausanias inveighs against the fathers of good-looking boys, who try to guard them from the attentions of lovers. This same Pausanias is the lover of the playwright Agathon, and Plato portrays both of these high-class "beautiful people" with touches of effeminacy, shortsightedness, and selfishness.

It's commonplace among literary theorists of our day to say that those Greeks weren't aroused by sexual desire but by the lust for power. That's why men would do to boys what they would never suffer to have done to them. But unless we believe that Greek cities were full to the brim with deranged rapists, that explanation doesn't satisfy. It does not account for either the pedophilia or the contempt for adult homosexuality. To put it in a different way, the Greeks had a strong sense of the relationship between what was beautiful or decorous and what was right. That sense went awry in this case, no question. But the pedophilia of the Greeks is best seen as something that might happen to a boy on his way to becoming a man, in a society whose foundational political institution was not the court or the meeting hall but the *gymnasion*, the open-air field for the instruction of boys, athletic competition, physical training, political conversation, and the informal transaction of business. The Greeks had the right idea, that boys are boys, and boys become men, but they took a bad way to get to the goal, one that was consonant with the restrictions they placed upon their wives, and one that eventually led to the exhausting physical and moral corruption of the Greco-Roman world during the centuries of the Empire. The early Christians saw the connections quite clearly, which is why they set themselves apart from the licentiousness. They did not frequent houses of prostitution, they did not divorce, they did not kill their babies, and they did not engage in sexual perversion.

The point is that if you accept the unnatural, you accept everything on the route to the unnatural. If you accept a perverse evil, you have already accepted the "natural" evil. You can't accept a man's right to put a bullet in his neighbor's head for the fun of it, and then deny him his right to eat his neighbor for the vitamins and minerals. You can't accept a man's right to punish his child by pushing him off a cliff, and then deny him his right to punish the child by flogging. You can't accept a man's right to do a lewd thing with a woman, and then complain that he has no right to look at a picture of it. You can't celebrate the printing of obscenities, and then embark upon a crusade against insensitive speech. The argument *a fortiori* is relentless. It leaves you no quarter. You cannot live in half a jungle. You cannot poison the waters on Monday and expect your tea to be sweet on Tuesday.

So this is not a case of standing on a tuft of grass sticking out of the mud on the side of a very slippery slope, wondering what we will meet farther down. The slippery slope is not a fallacy when long human experience suggests predictable stages on the road from respectable hypocrisy or moral weakness to complete collapse. People and cultures really do rot by degrees. But I'm not suggesting right now where I think we will end. I am observing where we have already been. I'm not asking the reader to consider what will be the more degraded evil we will tolerate, but rather the less degraded evil we have already tolerated in principle. A person who smokes marijuana may not then go on to use heroin; a wife who flirts immodestly with her friend's husband may not then go on to take him to bed. But the person who uses heroin has no cause to condemn marijuana, and the adulteress has no cause to condemn immodesty.

Above the biological and logical impossibility of same-sex "marriage," above mimic marriage, must lie what is biologically and logically possible, though defective or corrupt; just as bad food is more nutritious than iron filings or whatever else can only mimic food by our pretending to eat it. The most obvious and culture-destroying thing that is above us on the slope, that we have already passed and implicitly approved, is polygamy.

Consider the things that polygamy has going for it. It is conceivable. A man cannot mate with another man; the requisite organs are lacking. He cannot engage in matrimony with anyone but a woman who can become a mother, or who might have become a mother had circumstances permitted it. That is what matrimony means, after all. He can breathe on his own, he can take nourishment on his own, but he cannot engage in the marital act on his own, nor with another man. Only in the marital act do two human beings unite biologically as one, the organs in concert with one another in the act that is reproductive in kind. So a man cannot marry a man, and a woman cannot marry a woman, for all that they may try to pretend, as I may pretend to occupy two bodies at once, or to fly by flapping my arms; my view of the matter does not alter the reality. But a man *can* marry two women, or three, or twelve. He *should not* do it; it involves a deeply defective view of marriage. It violates the full meaning of the self-surrender implied by the union of the sexes. But it is at least *possible*.

No previous culture has ever blessed the mock-marriage of a man and a man or of a woman and a woman. But plenty of cultures have accepted polygyny, the marriage of one man to several wives. Certain religions allow it or encourage it: Islam allows a man to have up to four wives, and radical Mormonism is, as I understand it, even more generous.

There are reasons for it, such as they are. A rich man can thereby father and support dozens of children; the tribe benefits from the fecundity. A man can beget several children virtually at once. An older and well-established man can continue to father children long after his first wife has grown too old. If the first wife is barren, she need not be tossed aside, adding injury to her misfortune. If the children of the first wife die, the couple need not remain without support in their old age. The second wife may come as a relief to the first wife, and not as a sexual rival; the older woman may prefer that to a husband's roving with whores or lavishing attention and money and time on a secret mistress. I'm not arguing that polygamy is right. It is defective, and for us would mark a dreadful reversion to barbarism. As I say, it is culturally common; not as common as monogamy, but common enough not to surprise.

What grounds could we have to deny people the opportunity to marry more than one person? If we establish as a matter of law that marital relations are free to any two people who consent, why limit the number to two? Polygyny, after all, is much easier to justify than are homosexual relations. It does not violate the biology of the people involved; it mitigates the risk of venereal diseases; it brings forth many children; it preserves the ideal of the union of male and female. And please, no appeal here to "tradition" or to "what everybody knows." The former has been flouted, and the one thing that anybody who has ever been around a farmyard knows is that a male cannot mate with a male, and a female cannot mate with a female. And, sure enough, we are already hearing calls from threesomes and foursomes to allow it. After all, the bisexual should not have to limit his choice to one sex or the other, should he? Not if he can find a couple who will agree to the perverse arrangement.

At this point I have met two common responses. One is to relocate the evil of polygamy. The objector, wishing desperately to pretend that mimic-marriage is conceivable and good, but that polygamy is not, cannot object on the grounds of sex. That road has been blocked. Instead he objects on the grounds of power. "In a polygamous relationship," he says, "one of the wives would inevitably be subservient to the other," and, since Equality is the great empty idol of the modern world, even a hint of subservience must be abominated. These are, of course, the same people who submit supinely to a State that claims competence in everything from the prosecution of wars to the education of small children to the milking of cows to the polite content of a graduation speech to the price of a visit to the doctor. The worship of Equality, in practice, means deference to the Knowledge Class, people of high cranial capacity who combine nihilism with a boundless desire to reduce all human affairs to their managerial wisdom.

But do we really know for a fact that there must be subservience within the polygamous arrangement? Is it really inevitable? And if it is inevitable, why is that necessarily bad? Isn't there usually a dominant personality in any human relationship? And what if all parties involved accept either the risk or the fact? Suppose one of the wives should answer, "I believe I am *meant* to serve, and cannot feel fulfilled without serving." For her, that she is the secondary wife would be a cause for contentment, not envy. What can we say in reply? That she does not know her own mind? But that is another road we have blocked, since we have assumed that in sexual matters no one is ever self-deceived, so long as they can attribute some reason or other to what they want. It is absurd to approve of the sadistic toys sold at gay shops and during Yale's Sex Week, and then to grow strangely puritanical about a woman's professed desire to do most of the cleaning and cooking. It is absurd to smile at the orgies that gay men celebrate, and then to condemn Moroni on his ranch in Cedar City, with Leah in one bedroom and Rachel in another.

Nor can we call a self-professed secondary wife mad. If sanity is the mind's right response to what is real (*adaequatio mentis ad rem*), then if a man pretends he is a woman he is to that extent not sane, no more than if he pretends to be Julius Caesar, a horse, or an alien from an alternate universe. So we can hardly accuse the second wife of insanity, when at least she *is a wife*. But in any case, we have blocked that road, too. The Supreme Court decision *Casey v. Planned Parenthood* has already elevated sexual nihilism to the First Commandment of our anticulture. Each of us is entitled, in the misty words of Justice Anthony Kennedy, to determine for ourselves the meaning of the universe. That must imply that there is no meaning to be had; for even Anthony Kennedy would not claim that freedom entails our determining for ourselves the laws of gravity. If we accept what he says, all moral reasoning regarding the essence of sexuality is foreclosed from the outset. We can only reason about attendant circumstances, such as when a young person may properly consent to sexual activity. But about the thing itself, we must hold our peace. We must be sexual islands unto ourselves. This is a contradiction in terms, since sex is nothing if not interpersonal. If a society can have nothing to say about its most fundamental personal relations, then it may as well give up the notion that it is free and self-directing, and instead resign itself to the direction of advertisers, celebrities, the lusts of the most selfish and foolish among us, and the ambitions of those who will be in the political position to manage, and to profit by, the chaos that must result.

The second response I meet is the shrug. "What difference does it make to me?" says the objector, taking a swig on his beer and flicking the remote control for his television. "I'll love my wife all the same. I don't care what other people do. Let them do as they please."

And again we must return to the principle that we all live in the same place, we drink the same water, we breathe the same air; and therefore there can never be an individual "right" to do what would corrupt or destroy the very society within which that right is to be exercised. Civic liberty is for human flourishing and life, not for decay and death. So we must ask what would be the consequences, practical and moral, of opening the gates to polygamy.

I say that we would find ourselves in a world utterly different from the one into which we were born. One might say, "I do not believe in it; I will never marry another." But what about one's spouse? "I trust my husband!" she replies. "My wife isn't like that!" says he. But in part what makes the woman certain that her husband would never think of taking a second wife is that he and she have been brought up in a culture in which the very thought rouses disgust. The law is a teacher. If the law turns about and says, "There's nothing really wrong with taking a second wife," then at the very least it has removed a strong curb against bad behavior. What the law declares permissible, after many centuries of cultural rejection, will inevitably be celebrated by its proponents as a positive blessing, as has happened for fornication, divorce, abortion, and sodomy. I daresay that the history of the last hundred years shows how quickly what was once unthinkable—such as the State-sponsored incarceration and the murder of innocent civilians in a supposedly enlightened nation—can become a matter of course, in the blink of an eye, when the moral and religious guardrails are knocked over. No, if polygamy were allowed, it would not take long, it might not even take a month, before three glamorous movie stars or singers announced their polyamorous marriage, with the media following along in breathless vicarious delight.

How would the world change, then? For starters, it would render marriage porous as a matter of principle. It would instantly, first in law and then in cultural expectations, turn every married person into an eligible bachelor or bachelorette. The ring that you see on the man's finger means nothing, because he has a few more fingers without rings on them. The woman who is holding her husband's hand has another hand that is free. The woman who pursues a married man need not think of herself as a homewrecker. She comes not to wreck the home, but to install herself in it. She comes not to supplant, but to support. So at least she may justify the evil she proposes. The man who is in love with his best friend's wife may now make a "reasonable" proposition to him, and if he refuses, well then, all bets are off. Polygamy may easily be offered as the "compromise" between marriage and divorce, or between one marriage and another.

I am not engaging in wild suppositions here, but merely applying to this fundamental alteration of social life what we should have learned from past alterations. I'll discuss divorce more specifically in the next chapter, but the move to no-fault divorce was not supposed to change the number of divorces in any appreciable way. It was supposed to ease the burden from people who were going to divorce in any case. Instead it made divorce a live possibility, a relatively easy out. It "taught" people to look for that exit ramp; and so the divorce rate surged to what only a few years before would have been considered unimaginable levels.

More devastating than what no-fault divorce taught, though, was what it failed to teach. As I've been saying, whenever something is missing that should be there, it is hard to persuade people to look for it; most people lack either the historical knowledge or sufficient imagination to "see" the good things that a bad custom or a bad law has prevented from developing in the first place. The lax divorce laws failed to teach, or undid the teaching, that a marriage vow is a marriage vow, and that the promise of permanence is not meant to be conditional upon one's transitory feelings, or upon the money in the bank, or upon health or the satisfaction of one's ambitions as regards work or physical pleasure or social status. It is meant to be permanent. Or so it was; but in short order, once the guardrail was down, and once the permanence of the vow was denied as a matter of public principle, those words "till death us do part" and "as long as you both shall live" were rendered nugatory, merely ceremonial. They are the sorts of things people say, but do not really mean; for it is self-contradictory to say, "I will promise myself to you forever, for now."

I've said that it is possible for a man to marry two women. What's not possible, however, is for a man to marry two women *in the same way* in which he would marry one woman, with the same meaning. It is nonsensical to say, "I will give myself wholly to you, Mary, and also to you, Agnes, and also to you, Betty, and perhaps also to some other woman who may come along." That is another contradiction in terms. And since the meaning of a word or a gesture is not determined by private interpretation, since language is essentially the work of a community, the culture that allows for polygamy *has already altered and debased the meaning of your own marriage*, regardless of your intentions at the time of the wedding. In a land where a business contract is only a piece of paper, the very nature of your entry into a partnership is radically different from what it would be in a land where contracts are considered sacred. We cannot vouch for someone else's feelings. We can only vouch for the words we have heard him speak and the deeds we have witnessed. If the words are empty and the deeds are merely ceremonial, then we can vouch for nothing at all.

Now let's say that the promoter of same-sex pseudogamy concedes the point as regards polygamy. Suppose he says, "Yes, from what you say, I see that there are good reasons to prohibit polygamous arrangements, reasons that have to do with the common good and the very essence of marriage." But that is to give away the ballgame. For then the principle undergirding the sexual revolution falls. That principle is simply that, so long as all the parties agree, what adults do sexually is their own business, about which the community has nothing to say, either by way of custom or by the laws that corroborate and invigorate those customs. If we deny that principle, then we may well return to questions regarding the whole range of sexual actions once considered immoral, destructive of the self and of the common good. In that case we will be re-examining all kinds of crimes or sins against marriage. We'll reconsider other forms of mimic-marriage, such as when a man and a woman shack up, or when a woman uses a male "friend" to become pregnant. We'll look again at the madness of supposing that a person can declare himself to be ready to do the child-making thing, without the slightest intention to provide a permanent home in marriage wherein the child-to-be-made shall dwell. We'll look again at the harm caused to the common good by the shell game of contraception, which allows people to pretend that they are not doing what they are doing, and which robs from upright but weak-willed young people their main guard against aggression and heedlessness and enticement from the opposite sex. In other words, once the principle is denied, we have a great host of other, more fundamental, things to justify or to discourage or to condemn. Fraud can't be all right if breaking a vow is wrong. If it's wrong—if it hurts those who engage in it, and also the common good—for an unmarried man and woman to pretend that they are married, then we can forget about the two unmarried men.

I've said that polygamy is above us on the slope, and that we simply haven't noticed it or admitted it. Is there anything next to us on the slope, or beneath us, to which we have committed ourselves unwittingly?

Again, the slippery slope is a fallacy if, in a series of elements, the succeeding ones do not flow inevitably from the others, either as effects from causes, or as logically inevitable. We can't say that the man who begins by breaking the Sabbath is going to end by killing priests. But we can say that the man who justifies murder justifies slavery also, since both murder and slavery spring from the same evil principle, that human life is not sacred, and that we may use or abuse the lives of others as we see fit. Opponents of abortion have long claimed that there is no moral difference between killing a child in the womb and killing a child outside it, and that only a residual sentimental disgust prevented the more obvious infanticide. And now there are proponents of the abortion "right" who say exactly the same thing. Notice, I am not saying that a particular person who snuffs out the life of an unborn baby will himself undoubtedly snuff out the life of the baby in the crib. I am saying that the logic of evil has a life of its own, and will play itself out as far as it can until it is torn up by the roots.

If you say that a marriage is whatever the adults in question make it to be, then why should not a man marry his sister? Here we cannot appeal to attendant circumstances. We cannot say, "It is wrong because the children to be born might have birth defects." That's quite immaterial. We do not prevent blind people from marrying, simply because their children might also be blind. And, for all we know, the brother and sister may intend to crush or dismember or dissolve any children they conceive; and we have already given that our blessing. For all we know, the brother may have had a vasectomy, or the sister a hysterectomy. What then?

It's the mark of an intellectually stunted people that we cannot answer such a question. The proponents of same-sex pseudogamy cannot answer it, since the only possible answer involves both the rejection of the principle of the sexual revolution, and the recovery of the essential nature of two different kinds of relationship. We condemn incest—which word, interestingly enough, originally means simply unchastity, impurity, filth—because we recognize the precious nature of the relationship of parent and child, or of the relationship of brother and sister, and we protect these relationships from sexual confusion. The man who marries his sister (and again we are talking about what is at least biologically possible) does violence to the meaning of brotherhood and sisterhood, and to the meaning of matrimony, and to their interrelationship.

The law against incest codifies our moral disgust against mingling sexual activity into the close and intensely personal relations that brothers and sisters and mother and father must have, living together. A mother who washes her little boy in the bathtub is doing an ordinary thing. The brothers who jump naked in the pond together are doing an ordinary thing. The big brother who gives his little sister a hug and a kiss, or who tickles her, or who marches out of the bathroom with a towel around his waist, shouting, "Sis, where did you put the shampoo?"—he's just an ordinary brother. The mutual understanding that brothers do not marry sisters and parents do not marry children clears the space for these relationships to develop normally, without a shadow of doubt that a kiss may "mean" more than it should.

Moreover, we call "incestuous" any relationship among people who are unhealthily preoccupied with one another, to the exclusion of others outside the small group. The brother and sister who marry have closed their little family circle against other families, those that they should marry into. It is a weird kind of self-love and self-abuse. Marriage is the foundation of a community, by the interrelationships it develops; it is not the collapse of the community into a tiny inert atom of helium.

Again, it is not possible for same-sex pseudogamists to admit that certain human relationships have an essential nature which we must observe, a nature that is both biological and anthropological, and then deny the force of biology and anthropology in their one case. On the grounds they have proposed to justify the pseudogamy of a man and a man, *they must justify the real marriage of a brother and a sister.* If they admit that no sexual relationship among adults is justified by mere consent alone, then they are on my turf, and must argue accordingly.

What other clumps of weed in the mud are sprouting near us on the slope?

Prostitution is consensual. Why not? Strip clubs, same thing. Pornography, same. Bath houses for orgies, same. Every single objection to these things on grounds other than the moral— that these things are in themselves *wrong*, that they debase the people who participate in them, they coarsen the culture, they corrupt public morals, and help to destroy the family and the healthy relations between men and women—may be dispensed with. We can mandate vaccinations and periodic exams to obviate the direct risks to public health. We can distinguish between legal and state-overseen prostitution and the abuse of women on the streets. We can allow whores to unionize to help fix minimum wages and antiseptic working conditions.

What we *cannot have*, as I've said, is half a jungle. We can't have the world in which men and women love one another and raise healthy families, with almost all children born within wedlock and almost all children living with both parents, and their children in turn visiting their still-married grandparents, if at the same time we welcome the rest of the chaos. You can't have a child-friendly and marriage-friendly street with a porn shop and a strip club on it. The principle that the sexual "fulfillment" of adults is trumps must bear fruit accordingly. It is too wild a thing to nip here and there. It has to be uprooted. It is unworthy of a civilized and self-governing people.

Seventh Argument

We Must Not Seal Ourselves in a Regime of Divorce

THE banquet is over, and the guests and the families have lighted the way home in a big parade. Some of them are bearing torches. Others are singing merry songs about what's going to happen tonight. Then the bride stops in front of the threshold to his house. He's gone before her, and stands as if waiting for her, with the door open. He gestures in a call of welcome. Her name is Flavia, and his name is Quintus, but for this moment they use the ceremonial names that their own parents used, and their parents before them, back into the immemorial past.

Ubi tu Caius, she says, *ibi ego Caia. Wherever you shall go, Caius, there I Caia shall go also.*

And he lifts her up over the threshold, and their wedded lives begin.

Let's look at that moment in the ancient Roman ceremony, and see what it reveals about matrimony.

Why do the bride and groom not use their own names? Why do they use the masculine and feminine forms of the same name?

The ceremony suggests to Caius and Caia, whatever their names may be, that they are doing the thing that founds the city itself. They are citizens, with the commonest of names; they see themselves as united with all the other Roman men and women who have done the same. The marriage isn't a private affair. It can't be, not when the family is the seedbed of the city. Piety to one's country flows from the piety one owes to father and mother and children. There are no gods of the city if there are no household gods first.

And why the same name? When the Pharisees asked Jesus under what circumstances a man might lawfully divorce his wife, He surprised them by disallowing the question. "Moses permitted a letter of divorce," He said, "because of the hardness of your hearts; but from the beginning it was not so." Jesus then cites the words of Genesis, before the Fall, to express the essence of matrimony, one that harmonizes exactly with the pagan Roman custom above. "Male and female He created them," He says, "and for this reason a man shall leave his mother and father and cleave unto his wife, and they two shall be one flesh."

One flesh—a new thing in the world. I will not ask the reader to defer to sacred Scripture. I'm noting that the pagans themselves understood marriage in much the same way. Flavia and Quintus may enjoy one another's company. We call that friendship. But matrimony is qualitatively different. When they marry, in the very act that consummates the marriage, they become Caius and Caia; male and female to one another; a union of complementaries; *one flesh*.

This isn't mysticism. It is a plain biological fact. Quintus can eat on his own. Flavia can breathe on her own. Their bodies can do on their own all things that bodies can do, with one most important exception. They cannot reproduce on their own. They cannot engage in the marital act alone, the act that is child-making in nature, even when not in effect. For that act, the flesh of the man and the flesh of the woman as man and as woman are needed, and each for the other: the male is for the female, and the female is for the male. This is a union that is unique in human life. It is a complex union of embodied differences—differences that are essential in the meaning of the marital act. He is the one who plants the seed, and she is the one who accepts it. He begets, and she conceives. They aren't just two different people. Identical twins are still different people. A gregarious talker and a quiet thinker are two different people. Men and women, however, are from the two different and complementary *kinds* of people, doing the thing which fulfills that complementarity. That is why they have both two names and one name. They could not claim to be Caius and Caia, to be really one flesh, unless they were in fact Caius and Caia, male and female, the man in his maleness for the woman, and the woman in her femaleness for the man.

And that explains the content of what the bride says. This again is not sentimentality. It is a vow of permanence, which the Romans took very seriously, at least until they adopted bad habits from the peoples they conquered as they built their empire. Why make that vow? Why does Caia say that she will be wherever Caius is?

When we meet somebody we like, and we pursue a friendship, we don't feel we need to ratify it with a permanent vow. We understand, first, that a person should have many friends, and that there may be degrees and kinds of friendship, too; the friends whose company we enjoy, the friends to whom we might go to talk about our troubles; the friends with whom we share the things that mean most to us, such as our religious faith. There's no need for me to say to my new friend, "Wherever you go, Quintus, I, Quintus, will also go." That would seem bizarre, as if I wanted to fold my identity into that of my friend. But that's not what friendship is. There is no "one flesh" union in friendship, and no exclusivity. My friend may be my *alter ego*, my *other self*, before whom I can speak my thoughts aloud, as

Cicero says. But he's not my *other half*. If I suggested as much to him, he might look at me as if I wanted not friendship but a kind of morbid possession, and he would rightly shy away from it.

The reason why Caia promises that she will go wherever Caius goes is that, in actual fact, they two are a new thing in the world. They are *one*. The marriage is in principle indissoluble. Two businessmen can get together to form a partnership, and then, when they tire of the business, they can dissolve it without recrimination, and each can leave with half of the assets. Friendship is not like that. There is no such thing as half of a whole friendship. But there is such a thing as a half-friendship, as it were. For "friendship" is something of an abstraction, used to describe a congeries of personal habits and feelings, and the habits and feelings may change. Friendship admits of more and less, and can fade, if the friends are separated from one another for a long time. But you can't be "more" married than you were when you first consummated the marriage. You can, certainly, grow in love; you can deepen your gratitude for your spouse; your marriage can flourish and express itself in children and grandchildren. But you are either married or you are not. There's no middle option. Feelings can be attenuated, but not the marriage itself. Breaking a marriage requires an act of violence; the one-flesh union can only be dissolved by being put to death.

But why shouldn't it be put to death? What makes this kind of union different from every other, in its relation to time?

I've discussed how Edmund Spenser's great wedding poem, the *Epithalamion*, places the marriage in a constellation of social relationships and the things of nature. What I haven't mentioned yet is that the poem is structured to show forth the intersection, in marriage, of time and eternity. Spenser divided it into twenty-four stanzas, one for each hour of the day. He ends each of the "day" stanzas with a call for the celebrants and witnesses of his marriage, his townsmen and friends, the girls and boys, the creatures of wood and dale, all to shout and sing so loud that "all the woods shall answer, and their echo ring." But precisely when, at the latitude in Ireland where his wedding took place, and on the summer solstice, the night would fall— Spenser has calculated the percentage exactly and reflected it in the line number of the turn—he tells us that night has fallen, and then the refrain instructs the guests to cease their singing: "The woods no more shall answer, nor your echo ring."

Those are only a few of the temporal features of the poem. I've said that there are twenty-four stanzas, but actually there are twenty-three and a fraction, the degrees of the earth's tilt upon its axis, providing us with the seasons, and their times of sowing and harvest. That last stanza is also an "envoy," a farewell stanza, and one which frankly admits its incompleteness. The poet says that he had wanted to give his bride a finer gift, but accidents prevented him, and so instead he will give her this poem, which will be *for short time an endless monument.* The word *endless* is chosen advisedly. Here is the twelfth and central stanza of the poem, when bride and groom stand before God and man:

Open the temple gates unto my love,
Open them wide that she may enter in,
And all the posts adorn as doth behoove,
And all the pillars deck with garlands trim,
For to receive this Saint with honor due,
That cometh in to you.
With trembling steps, and humble reverence,
She cometh in, before the Almighty's view;
Of her, ye virgins, learn obedience,
When so ye come into those holy places,
To humble your proud faces:

Bring her up to th' high altar, that she may
The sacred ceremonies there partake,
The which do endless matrimony make;
And let the roaring Organs loudly play
The praises of the Lord in lively notes;
The whiles, with hollow throats,
The Choristers the joyous Anthem sing,
That all the woods may answer, and their echo ring.

The central line of the whole poem is the fourteenth in this stanza, and the words in its center are *endless matrimony*. All of which prompts the question, why? Let's forget the easy appeal to tradition. Why should matrimony in all cultures be a sacred event? Why should it be regarded, at least in the ideal, as *endless*?

We do not invite the priest to bless a date to go golfing. We do not speak in cosmic terms about having lunch with a new friend. We do not sing hymns of gladness when we strike a business deal, or make a closing on a house. What is different here?

The only reason why mankind has celebrated marriages is that they renew the race; they bring forth new life, within the bounds of a holy vow. We have a keen sense that in marriage, as in birth and death, we arrive at the borderlands of our contingency. We know that we need not have come into being; we know that we will pass out of being, at least in this physical mode, in this world. For a human being, whose mind is *capax universi*, capable of apprehending all things individually and in their mutual relations, the experiences of birth and death must necessarily touch upon the cosmos, for indeed we may say that when the child arrives, a universe arrives; a mind like a church, whose inside is greater than its outside, who can imagine worlds such as never have existed, while the merely physical world cannot imagine him or even, once he is here, conceive of his existence as such. When the old man goes down to his grave, a world goes with him—the mystery of his being, his knowing, his thinking, and his loving, never on this side of the grave to be encountered again.

These are events that claim our awe, and matrimony is like them. That's not because of the feelings of the bride and groom, and not because of their intention, if all goes well, to persist in living with one another. It is *only because matrimony marks the new thing in the world, the one flesh union that makes for another new thing in the world, the child.* If a man and a woman marry and, because of physical debility, cannot conceive a child, they still do the child-making thing, and, though they are not the efficient causes of a child's coming to be, they are still *exemplary causes,* causes by way of example. Even children know this, as they instinctively will look upon a married man and a woman as a mother and a father, or a grandmother and a grandfather. But when a man and woman marry with the intention of thwarting the natural action of the marital embrace, we wish them well, we wish they might change their minds and welcome the new life; their marriage is parasitical upon the life-welcoming marriage, and if that were all that happened in marriage, a matrimony without a matron, there would be no reason for us to celebrate it and remember it, as we do those other liminal times of birth and death.

Matrimony is to be endless—hence the ring, that symbol of infinity, and gold, symbol of incorruptibility—because in the marital act, the man and woman each bring precious strands of human history together, from long ages past, and from their union may arise a child who will perhaps marry in turn and do the same. But this is more than animal reproduction, because we are more than animals. We are those beings, as I've said, who have apperceptions of infinity. By rights, by the sort of creatures we are, we ought to be born within the garden of a perpetual and sacred vow. We should not be the result of what Milton scornfully calls "casual fruition." We deserve an ancestral dwelling place, and a secure home, and the promise of the same for our own children in turn.

The exclusivity and the indissolubility of marriage imply one another. Why is this so? When a man gives himself wholly to a woman, or a woman to a man—*Ubi tu, Caius, ibi ego, Caia*—they give themselves precisely as those creatures who dwell in time but whose minds are not bound by time. I cannot say, "I give myself wholly to you, *for a while*," because that is a human contradiction. We alone of all the creatures grasp that we were born and that we will die. I cannot think of myself as an ephemeral creature flitting along a course of random change. When I see a photograph of myself as a little boy, I do not say, "That is a picture of the little boy who eventually developed into this man here, who, by the way, possesses only an instantaneous existence." I say, "That's a picture of *me*." I do not say, thinking of a day to come, that some half-stranger who will occupy the continuation of my current body will die. I say, "Someday *I must die*." We cannot give ourselves wholly without giving ourselves forever. In this sense, polygamy and divorce resemble one another, the one by a refusal to make a complete self-surrender *for the good of the spouse*, and the other by revoking that self-surrender in time. They are both, we might say, sins against infinity.

And what does this have to do with pseudogamy? And why should we care? What difference should it make to us, if half of all marriages end in divorce?

The biologically absurd notion that a man *can marry* a man is conceivable only now, after we have made the marriage vow strictly ceremonial. The man may be placing the ring on the woman's finger, but he and she have their free hands behind their backs, with the fingers crossed. They judge other "marriages" by their own, which, though it genuinely is a marriage in fact, is not quite a marriage in intention. It is all too often a late-arriving excuse for a big party, to celebrate not something that is about to happen (since, let's say, they have already been living together, and may have a child), not something that changes them utterly, but rather their feelings for one another. The marriage is an expensive and showy bit of punctuation for their love. It is no more sacred than a big cookout. But anybody can have a big cookout. Two men can have one, or two women, or two women and a man, or any permutation and combination of the sexes.

The corrosion works in the other direction also. Same-sex friendships, as I've said, do not produce any one-flesh union. They are by nature, not by circumstance, barren. Therefore they do not in themselves touch upon the eternal or the infinite. There is no reason in our embodied nature why a friendship should be either permanent or exclusive. Bill is not "cheating" on his friend Alan if he goes bowling with Ray. We still, even in our confused times, blame someone who ends a marriage seemingly without cause, but nobody blames someone who falls out of touch with a friend, or who eases away from the friendship because his interests have changed. And the behavior of homosexual men bears this out. Even when they pretend to marry, they do not feel any great need to keep themselves only to one another, as long as they both shall live. Homosexual activists instead insist that our notions of infidelity must change: an extramarital liaison does not qualify as infidelity, they say, if the other partner knows about it, or if the other partner does the like, or if the encounter is anonymous or momentary, or if the other partner himself takes part in it! And why should this assertion surprise us? For their relations *are not like* those between men and women, as a matter of physical and anthropological fact. They do not form the one-flesh union. Theirs is a sexualized friendship, and though it may well call up strong feelings, and though a man abandoned by his male lover may well feel miserable about it, the expectations regarding fidelity are quite different, as male homosexuals themselves candidly admit. The pseudogamous relations are only about as stable as any friendships would be, and not at all exclusive.

The problem again is that we do not form little friendship-islands or sex-partner-universes unto ourselves. It is absurd to believe, at one and the same time, that a man *can marry* a man, and that expectations regarding the fidelity of Adam and Eve to one another must be different from those regarding the fidelity of James and Robert. We cannot have things both ways. All marriages, in effect, will be regarded as pseudogamous, pretend-affairs that are valid so long as the feelings that prompted them persist, or so long as the partners (notice the disembodied language deriving from the business world) agree, but involving no reality outside their wills. Then if we must shrug when Robert goes hunting strange flesh after-hours, we have no reason not to shrug if Adam or Eve does the same. The go-ahead for casual adultery cannot reasonably be limited to the male homosexuals. In a sense, even with the best of intentions, Adam and Eve, though they can actually marry one another, will lose most of the cultural recognition of their marriage and the cultural support to help them through hard times. Nobody cares overmuch what happens to a private friendship, after all.

Here someone may say that we don't really have anything to worry about, since divorce rates in the United States at least have been leveling off and even falling. That's whistling in the graveyard. In the nineteenth century, when divorce rates began to swell as high as ten percent, both Protestants and Catholics were alarmed, and the Divorce Reform League was founded—to prevent lax divorce laws in one state from bleeding over into the others. Ten percent—not forty percent or fifty! That's a difference in degree that becomes a difference in kind. Ten percent is already bad. If ten percent of your soldiers do not obey orders, you have a deeply dysfunctional platoon. If ten percent of your customers filch things from your shelves, you'll find it hard to stay in business. If ten percent of your fifth graders still can't read *Tom Sawyer*, somebody ought to be fired. But if forty or fifty percent of your soldiers do not obey orders, you have no platoon at all, but chaos. Might as well disband the platoon, shutter the business, demolish the school.

So the news that divorce rates in America have eased from horrible to terrible is not great cause for rejoicing. But the divorce rate tells only a part of the story. When the Divorce Reform League was founded, almost everyone was married by age twenty-five, and almost all children were born within wedlock. Therefore the divorce rate provided a fair measure of social dissolution. It does so no longer. That's because in our time fewer than ten percent of the population are married by age twenty-five; marriages are not being formed in the first place. And forty percent of our children are born out of wedlock.

What we need, then, is an index of social dissolution. How many sexual relationships of any duration—say, one year—dissolve? How many of these failed relationships have produced children? We should not "protect" the numbers by ruling out of bounds all the other "divorces," some of them more socially disruptive than divorce proper. If we look at the whole picture, it resembles a bombed-out city, with here and there a house that has managed to survive intact, surrounded by twisted gates, half-smashed dwellings where people still eke out a life, cats and dogs gone feral, and wild, angry children kicking refuse amid the ruins.

Why should we care? I might at this point hurl the question back. How can we not care? Visit a prison someday, and ask the men there about their sexual history and that of their parents. Find out how many of them grew up without a father in the home. Find out how many have themselves fathered children out of wedlock, whom they do not now see. Sociologists rely upon numbers to show the dreadful harm wrought by all forms of divorce, both that which dissolves a marriage recognized by the State, and those which dissolve liaisons that are from their inception in a state of disorder. They can discourse all day long on rates—dropping out of school, depression, drug use, crime, teenage pregnancy, second-generation divorce, and so forth. One must have a heart of iron to pretend that all is fine, when children must suffer so badly for the selfishness of their parents; when children must be "grown up," so that their parents can persist in behaving like self-willed children.

The real harm, however, cannot be captured by numbers. No human thing can ever really be. What the divorce regime has done is to infect with transience what ought to be the most intimate and enduring of human bonds. It has eradicated from our minds the very idea of a complete and irrevocable self-donation. Most of us will never be called upon to brave the cannons of an enemy on the battlefield, or to rush into a burning building to save a child. Our calls to heroism must be of a less dramatic sort, but no less real, demanding more patience and self-sacrifice, and productive of more human good. It is easy to stand your ground when the enemy is far away. It is hard to do it when you are face-to-face. It is easy to balance your checkbook and avoid arguments about money when you are rich. It is hard to do it when every dollar counts, or when the electric bill has to wait a month while you scramble together the funds to pay the heating bill.

It is easy to be loyal when loyalty costs you nothing. But when the hard times come, as come they must; when conversation is strained, and even the bed brings no real pleasure; when the future seems but an interminable stretch of cloud and rain; then only the vow stands between marriage and divorce, and then it is that married couples most need the moral suasion and support of a genuine culture about them. To say, "We will not hold you to your vow" is to say, in effect, "You cannot really make a vow to begin with." But it is essential to our humanity to promise ourselves; we can only find happiness by giving away our pursuit of it; we know joy when we open ourselves up to its free arrival; it is better to be chosen than to choose. Many men and women in difficult marriages would learn these things eventually, if we did our duty by them and held them to their vows when they were weak. Many, knowing from the outset that a vow is a vow, will come to those conclusions naturally without the difficult lessons.

People will say, "The only marriages that would dissolve under lax divorce laws would have been miserably unhappy in any case." That's nonsense. In the divorce regime, the very meaning of marriage has changed; and the married couple have no overriding incentive from the start to set aside their selfishness and make the best marriage they can make. There's an exit sign on the back door. There will always be that phantasm of delights missed, or chances for fairy-land passing away. People seeking an excuse to dissolve the marriage will provoke reasons if none exists, or will plant themselves in stubbornness in order to exasperate what is already bad. Most divorces are secured for what people before our own time would have considered scandalously frivolous reasons—not physical cruelty, not adultery, but willfulness, irritability, and boredom. Then we set such people free—and divorces are more often than not sought by the party most to blame; the greener-grass seeker, the golddigger, the unreliable, even the adulterous. They then may go on, like carcinogenic free radicals in the body politic, to corrupt yet another household, rather than to have their self-will cordoned off in one household and, possibly, healed by the long-suffering and kindness of the spouse, or by simple maturation. At the worst they would be able to say, "I kept my promise, and our children and our children's children visit us together, and if we could not be excellent spouses to one another, at least we did not make them suffer the pain of divorce." And now, if those children marry, they will have an example of perseverance to guide them through the straits they will meet in turn.

But the principal social effect of the divorce regime is not what happens within the marriage. It's what happens in general to all social institutions. The transience infecting the heart will not remain within the quarantine of the house. All things once enduring must become transient also. Neighbors will not know one another, because the more fundamental human relationship cannot be relied upon; boyfriends and girlfriends come and go. If a spouse cannot be trusted with a sacred vow, a townsman certainly cannot be trusted with much less. The habit of committing oneself to a neighborhood, a business, a school, or a town never forms. We are left with chaos and alienation at the local level, mass-management above, and infidelity—the implicit sin of the self-serving—all throughout.

And this, too, is something that the pagans understood. Consider the word *integrity*. It does not mean sincerity; that and a really fine pumpkin patch won't get you much. The man of *integrity* is integrated. He does not make his moral decisions *ad hoc*, reckoning up advantages, or gauging his feelings. He sees, too, that all of the virtues are related to one another, and are meant to inform the whole life of a man. He therefore would no more cheat a customer than he would commit adultery. He would no more lie under oath than he would flee from his post in time of war. He would no more spread rumors about his enemy than he would sprinkle rat poison upon a beggar's dish. His honesty is brave; his chastity is generous; his great-heartedness is clean. But the divorce regime teaches and rewards dis-integrity. And one can no more build a great nation or even a good, solid town upon dis-integrated people, than one can build a town hall out of straw, or a church out of dust.

Again, the evil principle is that the sexual gratification of adults must be met; no customs or laws may stand in its way. The principle is a universal solvent. Nothing can contain it.

Eighth Argument

We Should Not Normalize an Abnormal Behavior

T HERE'S a scene in *Tom Sawyer* that must warm any man's heart who remembers what it was to be a boy.

Tom and Huck and a couple of their friends have gone on a day-long outing. They've smuggled from town a lot of bacon and bread and other things to eat, and they've clambered aboard a canoe hidden in the thickets on their side of the Mississippi, near the cave where they've met and sworn blood brotherhood and vowed to kill the kin of any of the boys who rats on the others or spills their secrets. At first it looked as if Huck wasn't going to be allowed in as a brother, because he hadn't any kin, but Huck reminded them of the widow he sort of lived with, and the boys, with a sigh of relief, said it was all right then, they could kill the widow instead.

So they've rowed the boat out into the Father of Waters, to one of the islands near the other shore of that mighty river. And there they play at being pirates, Tom being Black Tom of the Spanish Main. After an hour of running and hollering and killing and being killed, they strip and jump in the water and swim. Then they lie down on the sand, absolutely exhausted. Then comes bacon roasting on a fire.

What appeals to us about their boyish antics? And what's wrong with Tom's brother Sid, the effete snob who would never be caught dead doing such a thing?

We sense right away that the boys are doing something that boys of any gumption and imagination would do. It may not have been common even in Mark Twain's time. But it was *normal*—it was a healthy and imaginative and spirit-raising and body-toughening exercise of boyish initiative. And *normal* girls like my wife, who loved the book when she was Tom's age, respond to it too, because *they like boys.*

Right away I must defend the use of the word *normal.* Before I do, I beg the reader to admit that it is madness not to consider that some things are normal and some are not. If a ten-year-old child runs away in a fright whenever a dog passes by, that is not normal. Something's wrong with the child, and his parents ought to do what they can to help him overcome the fear. If a married woman of modest means spends more money every month on makeup than she does on food for her baby, there is something wrong here, too, and she needs to see either her confessor or a psychiatrist, or perhaps both. If a group of adults on bicycles rides into the middle of a park in broad daylight, stark naked, when they know well that children are going to be there, there's something wrong with them. They too should see a confessor, and a psychiatrist, and the inside of the local jail.

If a teenager is so terrified of gym class that she retches and breaks out into a cold sweat, then something is very wrong with her or, far more likely, with the class itself. If a man cannot take home his weekly paycheck without feeding a quarter of it into a keno machine, he has been warped by a destructive habit. Our language reveals a great deal here. When something is *wrong*, it is literally bent out of shape, *warped*, twisted, perverse. You can't build a house with twisted walls. You won't make friends if your speech is not straight. No one would trust a doctor unless he was a man of professional *rectitude*, who did things in the *right way*. Everyone admires the rare politician who is *straightforward*, whatever his beliefs may be. But the mayor who fixes bids on construction projects so that they will be won by his friends and relations, while he skims the cream from the top for himself? He's *crooked*.

The word *normal* is like those. I am well aware of the vulgar notion, peddled by teachers from kindergarten to the doctorate, that the normal is only a matter of statistical frequency. This is to confuse two very different concepts. We may say, rather imprecisely, that it was *normal* for Nazi officers of the SS to round up Jews and other enemies of the all-competent Reich, herd them into trains, haul them to concentration camps, and then subject them to unimaginable brutality, including slaughtering them by the hundreds with poison gas. When we say that, all we mean is that a lot of SS officers did those things. It was common in that nasty corral. But in a deeper sense, in the more precise sense of the word, it was not *normal* at all. It was the manifestation of a national psychosis. It was the backup of a sewer of evil. It went a long way toward proving the existence of a spiritual evil far beyond even the capacious imagination of man to invent on his own.

The word derives from the Latin *norma, carpenter's square*. You use a *norma* so that your walls will be at *right angles*—note the adjective—to the floor. If they aren't at right angles, they might cave in or buckle out. The poet Lucretius, commenting on the life of man, says that if you begin with false principles, you will be like a man whose straightedge is crooked and whose *norma* is out of square. You'll try to build a house, but the thing will fall apart. You won't have built according to *rule*—according to the nature of your materials and the obvious requirements of floors and walls and roofs.

What is normal, in this sense, is, to use other phrases, as right as rain, well-balanced, straight as an arrow, on an even keel. It doesn't imply that every boy, let's say, will be exactly like every other boy, no more than will all houses or boats be exactly the same. But all houses fit for human habitation will have to use materials like wood and stone in a way befitting their natures and the ordinary uses we have for houses. And we don't build boats out of granite.

If we see a boy who skulks whenever his father enters the room, we may suspect that the child is abnormally shy, or the father is distant or cold or brutish, or the mother has spoiled the child and interfered with his healthy identification with the father. Something there is *wrong*, psychologically, and perhaps also morally. We understand that it shouldn't be. His fear should be allayed. That relationship needs to be set *right*, with gentle love—perhaps with a couple of weeks in the country, away from mommy. If we see a teenage girl who cannot talk to boys, and cannot even talk to most other girls, but who fixes upon one girl alone, her best and only friend, smothering her with attention and preventing her from reaching out to others of both sexes in a healthy and ordinary way, we see again that something is *wrong*, and someone with more experience than they have should try at least to introduce a third and a fourth girl into that too-tight circle.

And what then do we make of a young man who feels revulsion in front of girls, or who wants desperately to be a girl—wants to be Catherine Earnshaw, with Heathcliff crying out for him in the night? What about a nine-year-old boy who is persuaded that he is a girl and wants to dress up as one? Or a boy who hates his own sex and wishes he were rid of it? Or one who hangs around the bathrooms at the local gym, eyeing up the guys in the shower in the hopes that one of those nameless men will give him the signal back? There's no balance here, no equable approach to reality. Something has gone wrong. We're looking at a failure to grow into a healthy acceptance of one sex or the other or both.

I hear the howls of protest. But I am only saying what every man knows in his heart to be true. I can't speak for women; some of them may find male behavior in general to be incomprehensible or even appalling. I'll say without fear of contradiction that no sane father of a son wants anything other for his boy than that he should grow up with a healthy acceptance of his sex, comfortable around other boys and men, attractive to girls and attracted to them in turn; and that he will, if he finds a good woman who will take him, marry and have children in turn. It is perfectly natural. It is right as rain. It is what all good fathers and mothers have always wanted—and they are right to expect others about them, teachers, coaches, priests, parents, and counselors, to confirm them in this expectation, and to do nothing that might lay a snare in their son's path. The same goes for girls. I'd warn my daughter away from any touchy-feely teacher who preaches the feminist poison that women need men as fish need bicycles. Cast your net somewhere else, Frustrata.

It hardly needs mentioning that the male and female bodies are made for one another, in the obvious ways, and in more subtle ways which medical science is only beginning to discover. (A humorous instance: biologists say that the pheromones from a man's sweat have a calming effect upon a room full of women. My wife firmly denies that this is so.) Before the current wave of political advocacy, many psychologists who studied homosexual men did arrive at some plausible conclusions about the same-sex attraction. The crucial figure, again and again, is the father. T. E. Lawrence was an illegitimate son whose father ignored him. Rock Hudson's father left his mother when he was eight, and the boy had a troubled youth, raised by her and her parents. Raymond Burr's parents separated when he was a boy, and he too was raised by his mother and her parents. Tab Hunter came from a broken home with an abusive father. Montgomery Clift's father was violent and abusive, so the boy left home at age thirteen to work on Broadway; his first long-term sexual relationship was with a middle-aged woman, a cradle robber. By age thirty, Clift was a physical wreck, addicted to alcohol, pills, and chloral hydrate. Whenever Montgomery Clift wanted to impersonate someone in a mad rage, he imagined his father.

I believe male homosexuals when they say they have always felt attracted to other males. There is no reason to doubt them on this. They believe that this attraction makes them different from their brothers—and this is where they go wrong. The plain fact is that all boys have a deep need (again, this is something hard to explain to women) for male acceptance and affirmation. All boys are attracted to the athletic, the popular, the gregarious, the cheerful, the clever boy, or man, as the case may be. This need is expressed in various ways: sometimes by shutting girls out of the club; sometimes by horseplay; sometimes by the violent high spirits of a gang; sometimes by initiation rites; sometimes by sworn devotion to a higher cause. In every boy there is a strain of that Tom Sawyer who organizes the other boys around him, or of the boys who look to a Tom Sawyer. The art of every culture testifies to these powerful (and difficult) friendships: *Gilgamesh, Huckleberry Finn, David Copperfield, Kidnapped, The Iliad, Star Wars.*

From this single assumption, all else follows. Suppose the boy has a cruel father, who makes fun of him for being slow or fat or clumsy. Or suppose he is naturally shy, and is rejected by the local boys—as he watches their rough games resentfully yet longingly from the kitchen window. Or suppose the boy's older brothers ignore him, and he watches in envy as they catch the football or flirt with the pretty girl, while their father takes out all his many frustrations on him, the youngest. Suppose, when he's young, he's funny-looking and is teased ruthlessly by both boys and girls, and grows painfully introverted. Suppose his father runs out on his mother, and she marries again, and the stepfather hates the child. Suppose he's young and talented, and his hard-driving father forces him to work a hundred hours a week to support the family. Suppose he's shy and soft-bodied and his father won't ever leave him alone, but has to make him into the athlete he's never going to be, and embarrasses him constantly in front of other boys. Suppose his father dies when he's twelve and he ends up raised by his mother and his sister, in a hick village where he has nothing in common with anybody. Suppose his father shoots himself in the head when the boy is eight, and the mother marries a man the boy loathes. I've derived all of these examples from real people's lives. Half of them I've known personally. Imagine a boy who is rejected by the most important males in his life. The longing for male companionship does not go away; and remember, the boyish friendship is expressed with an active and frank physicality. Why shouldn't it be? There's everything in the world *normal* about the scenes in the pleasant movie *Breaking Away,* when the four working-class boys are hanging around the abandoned quarry for diving and swimming, or when they ride together as a relay team for the annual bicycle race, and they defeat the college boys and win the cheers of the ordinary people in town. Those scenes are absolutely as normal as those when the protagonist of the movie, the only one of the four who goes to college, pretends to be an Italian in order to serenade and woo the pretty freshman girl; or when one of his friends takes his high school sweetheart to the justice of the peace to secure a marriage license. The camaraderie of boyhood and its foibles are sometimes glorious, sometimes raucous, sometimes solemn, sometimes hilarious.

It's what should happen naturally for every boy. Now suppose that snares have been laid in the boy's path.

What happens now may depend on other factors. He may enjoy the company of some one friend in whom he can trust, or a loving father who will make rejection by the other boys pale in importance. He may latch onto another group of boys who share his interests, computer graphics or chess or music. He may luck out physically, suddenly growing taller and stronger than the boys who once snubbed him. Failing that, the boy must struggle on his own to define himself as a boy, or must accept that he "deserves" to be rejected by the others, because he is not a real boy. This struggle is for the central fact of the boy's existence. That too is unwittingly supported by homosexuals, who alone among people of all kinds of sexual habits associate their very identities with their longings.

When the boy reaches puberty, the longing assumes a new character, influenced by the boy's new capacity for sexual arousal and his developing, and often chaotic, feelings of sexual desire. The same kind of bodily fooleries that help form the identity of other boys become for him moments of great dread, or desire, or both at once. Hence the compulsiveness of the homosexual's behavior. Like other compulsives, he scratches at a wound that will not heal; he visits again and again the painful memory; he aches to fulfill a longing whose source he can no longer rightly recognize. Most boys pestered by these feelings grow out of this silly stage; the homosexual, who was denied the chance to undergo it in the normal way, returns to it as if compelled. And there is a strong element of obsession and compulsion in his behavior. Temperance alone will suffice for a normal man to refrain from going to bed with a woman to whom he is not married. He can go play a round of golf, or climb a mountain, or do something else that will distract him. Much more than temperance is required of the man who has yielded to an abnormal habit. That is why the name of the Catholic organization for the spiritual assistance of homosexual men (and women) is not Temperance or Continence. It is *Courage*.

What the male homosexual longs for, sexually, is what every male needs: affirmation by other men—and then, when that is secured, the love of a woman who will allow him to be a man, and not mother him to death. He has to know that he belongs, he's a man, he can be relied on in a fight, he has what it takes; and then, that there's a good woman for him, not an insatiable devourer of his time and his energy, manipulative and abnormally dependent at once. If a boy is given this affirmation, he will not become a homosexual, unless he is attacked directly and thereby made to doubt the authenticity of his manhood— that is, unless he's been raped or seduced by another male on the lookout to pick off the most vulnerable of the herd. This too is a plain fact: it is a sufficient condition for the nonappearance of the syndrome. If a father affirms his son physically (for the rough touch of a good father's love is never forgotten by the son), the son will identify with the father. He will know he is a boy, to follow his father in marrying a woman and having children by her.

Thus male homosexuality is a corruption not of the relations between men and women, but of the relations between men and men. It is an aberrant eroticization of male friendship. And that explains the staggering promiscuity. Male homosexuals don't want to admit this, but they all know men who have had relations with hundreds of other men, many of them anonymous, almost all of them casual. It doesn't mean that they are callous by nature. What a man seeks in a woman is not what he seeks in a man. Husband and wife may be "friends," but they are also less and more than that. My wife is not an alter ego; we do not stand side by side to conquer the world. But I find in her what I lack in myself. She is the mysterious one who is not like me; and my love for her is quite unlike my love for my friend, who is like me. There is nothing casual about marriage, but friendship descends from the summit all the way down to pleasant and passing acquaintances. If it is friendship that male homosexuals seek, then we might predict many of their otherwise inexplicable behaviors. Friendship is not exclusive; one can never have too many friends; friendship is often celebrated best in boisterous groups; to live even a week or two without the feeling that one has a friend is agonizingly lonely.

What's more, the homosexual knows better than anything that something has gone *awry* with him. Hence his now enthusiastic adoption of the word *queer*. That word too, in its origin, suggests something out of kilter, running crosswise. If you have a *queer feeling* in your stomach, you might look again at the stuff on the plate to make sure it was cooked well enough. If you have a *queer feeling* about the realtor who is trying to sell you a house, you may suspect that he isn't being straight with you about that very old heater in the basement, or about the little termite damage you've noticed under the eaves. The whole point of *Queer Theory* in our universities is to persuade students to accept the abnormal as normal, and to see supposedly abnormal strains underneath the normal. Transgression used to be synonymous with sin. Now, in the language of the Queer Theorists, it denotes the courageous crossing of a boundary which the rest of society draws arbitrarily to justify itself and cast out the "other." Transgression—or, to use the fancy lingo, "the transgressive"—is something to celebrate.

This position is riddled with contradictions. Professor Smith, confronting a student who plagiarized his paper on the transgressive protest, would unquestionably not congratulate him for overstepping the boundary between "my work" and "somebody else's work." Professor Jones, walking back to his car after a conference on the transgressive in contemporary rap music, would be duly appalled to find that a fatherless kid on the streets had transgressed the boundary of his windshield, with a hammer. Professor Brown, having spent the day at school celebrating the transgressive humor of rioters in the sixties, who employed the uproarious slogan "Off the Pigs" to recommend killing policemen with wives and children—I shall give the reader a moment to recover from his laughter—discovers that his auto mechanic has transgressed the boundary between their bank accounts, overcharging him fifty dollars for his new transmission. Professor Brown proceeds to read him the riot act.

It would be absurd to suppose that we must draw boundaries between what is right and wrong, or between what is good, what is not good but to be tolerated, and what is wicked, in all areas of human behavior *except in the single area most determinative of human culture.* It would be like saying that retail merchants must be honest, but executives of large corporations may rob their stockholders blind. Then the question is not whether such boundaries are to be drawn, but where and why, according to what moral and pragmatic principles, and with what effect upon the common good.

Another thing that's odd about the homosexual's self-designation as "other" is that he has in a most fundamental way denied the obvious *other* in human life. The theorists sneer at the plain fact that a man is made for a woman and a woman for a man, and call it "heteronormativity," with the sense that it is a wicked and bigoted thing for fathers and mothers to expect their boys to marry girls and their girls to marry boys. But what those perfectly normal children are doing is crossing the very gulf that the homosexuals have not managed to cross, and sometimes have not dared to try to cross. The normal children are not stuck on their own sex, like adolescents in neutral. The men actually love women. The women actually admire men. The men can cheerfully celebrate the courage of a Joan of Arc, without envy. The women can watch a movie like *On the Waterfront*, and actually feel gratified that the only prominent woman in the movie is loved by the ex-boxer and helps to bring about his moral conversion. They, the normal, are the people who can best advise us on how to accept into your life the strangest and most routine-upsetting creature in the world—somebody of the opposite sex. And that's before the newborn child invades the hardly settled home and takes it by storm.

Finally, the justifier of what is "queer" cannot make up his mind whether it is queer or not. It isn't possible to have things both ways. It cannot be ordinary on Monday and transgressive and bold and subversive and the rest of it on Tuesday. Which is it to be? If it is ordinary, why the Gay Pride parades, with lewd floats and signs, and men walking naked down the street or simulating sodomy in front of the crowds? The first time I ever saw something of the sort was when my family and I went to a yearly summer parade in Rhode Island, and along came a float with one man on it and a "bar" with a gay name. He was wearing bikini shorts and dancing to some reggae music. A sign read "Parking in Rear." The crowd fell as silent as stone. I turned my daughter's attention elsewhere. Normal people don't do things like that.

Most ordinary people who support the biological absurdity that a man can feasibly marry another man do not feel comfortable with sexual aberrancies. They wish to pretend that the one does not imply the other, and will point to the white house with the picket fence, where Ozzie and Harry live, who are at least on the surface "just like" everybody else, as if the man's failure to adjust to the reality of his body is like being left-handed, rather than like having succumbed to a serious psychological and moral disorder. But then they are left with a fact with no explanation, except that the people were "born that way"—born to have been abandoned by a father, born to have been molested, born to have suffered cruelty from boys. Nor does their position have any explanatory power in its own right. Being left-handed is uncommon but *normal*, in the sense that a lefty will still do with his hands all the things that the righty will do. Lefties also live in houses with straight walls. Lefties like right angles, too.

The very word *orientation* suggests, besides, more than what its promoters want it to. It does not mean that one faces this direction or that direction. If you are lost in the woods, you are*disoriented*; literally, you are not facing east, when east is where you want to be going, or east will tell you where the other *directions* are. The promoters want us to believe that one orientation is as right as another. That cannot be true. There are people now who say that they are *oriented* towards children; they are sexually aroused by little girls or little boys. Yes, that is a sexual *orientation*. There are some ideas that are so absurd, so divorced from reality, that only an intellectual can think himself into the pretzel requisite for justifying them. They will say, "Yes, this is an orientation," because according to their principles they must say so, "but we can draw a distinction between the orientation and acting upon it. The orientation is 'natural' for that person and must be tolerated, even though he should never, ever act upon it."

Sorry, it won't do. There is something psychologically and morally warped about somebody who seeks out pictures of little children undressed. Something has gone badly *wrong* there. It's not just a bad thing to act upon. It's a bad attraction to have. It is a *disorientation*. Why? I return to the obvious facts of nature. Children are not legitimate objects of sexual attraction, because they do not yet possess their sexes in their fullness. They, in their still childlike nature, cannot yet marry and have children. They are also in the crucial period of sexual latency, when their bodies and minds are developing so that someday they will be able to marry and have children, in well-adjusted and successful families. We rightly sense that there is something creepy about someone who would *want to invade that period of latency, even if he in fact does nothing about it.*

And will he in fact do nothing about it, absolutely nothing? That's not likely. I don't think it would be hard for us to see that such a person could never be entirely innocent around children. The hand on the shoulder that lingers too long, the gaze into the eyes, the hint of a suggestive jest, the unseemly preoccupations—no ordinary parent would want his child to hang around someone who had professed a sexual attraction to children. No more would he hire for his deceased spouse an undertaker who had professed an attraction to cadavers. These attractions themselves, and not just the attendant actions, are *wrong.*

Now if the failure to accept one's own sex in relation to the other sex is abnormal—not just uncommon, but out of kilter, awry, stunted, unbalanced—then we should expect the abnormality to show up in other ways, too. Homosexual men are common enough in San Francisco, where they enjoy tremendous political clout. Yet San Francisco is the very place where the efflorescence of the abnormality is most clearly manifest: nudism, public lewdness, sex shops, orgies, sadism and masochism, anonymous sex, and so forth. These are not what you get when you repress a healthy activity. These are what you get, en masse, when you promote an unhealthy activity. I'll have more to say about this in a later chapter.

Let me make clear that I'm not calling for jail time for Ozzie and Harry. I don't want to live in a police state. Such as we are, we can't have any measure of freedom if we try to uproot every evil. Some bad things require our tolerance. Not our approval, much less our promotion or celebration. To tolerate is to practice the virtue of forbearance. We are all of us weak in one way or another. Few are the saints among us. If we did not bear with the infirmities and the sins of our brothers, we'd not be able to get through a single day without an argument, and each of us could then build his own house apart from everybody else, where he could sit alone by the fire and fume about everyone's faults but his own.

Most men who find themselves compulsively attracted to other men have been brought to that pass by the cruelty or the neglect of others. They deserve our patience and our compassion. But the tolerance on our part requires from them an acknowledgement that we indeed do have something considerable to tolerate. From them, then, we rightly require discretion. We require that they not do to our children what may have been done to them. We require that they not burden others needlessly. They may do what they will in their homes. But that is no reason to flaunt it in the streets. That flaunting is a demand for social approval which, for all the reasons I've offered, we should not give, no more than we should give social approval to men and women who shack up, to divorcees, to pornographers, to porn users, to prostitutes, to adulterers, or to anybody else who violates the goodness of being male or being female.

Ninth Argument

To Celebrate an Abnormal Behavior
Makes Things Worse, Not Better,
for Those Inclined to Engage in It

LADY Macbeth has just received an urgent letter from her husband. He has revealed to her his good fortune in battle, and his having been hailed by three "weird sisters" as the future king of Scotland. King Duncan, a good and kindly ruler whose main fault is that he has placed his trust too easily in unworthy noblemen, has made Macbeth the Thane of Cawdor and has promised to make him "full of growing." That's not enough for Macbeth, who wants to overleap Duncan's heir Malcolm and seize the crown for himself.

We have seen, so far, nothing in Macbeth to suggest that he is an evil man, and nothing to suggest that he is a particularly good man. But he is a *suggestible* man. He is prone to evil imaginations; that we have seen. His friend Banquo has also been greeted by the witches, but Banquo is not fascinated by them. He rather directs toward them an ironical and scornful wit—seeing even before they answer his question that there's something *wrong* with them, that they aren't what they should be:

Live you or are you aught
That man may question? You seem to understand me,
By each at once her chappy finger laying
Upon her skinny lips: you should be women,
And yet your beards forbid me to interpret
That you are so.

And when the witches turn their attention instead to Macbeth, hailing him three times as in a hellish ritual, first as the Thane of Glamis, which he is, then as the Thane of Cawdor, which he has become though he has not heard it yet, and then as king, Macbeth is visibly shaken. Banquo, however, maintains his composure:

Good sir, why do you start, and seem to fear
Things that do sound so fair? I' the name of truth,
Are ye fantastical, or that indeed
Which outwardly ye show? My noble partner
You greet with present grace and great prediction
Of noble having and of royal hope,
That he seems rapt withal; to me you speak not.
If you can look into the seeds of time
And say which grain will grow, and which will not,
Speak then to me, who neither beg nor fear
Your favors nor your hate.

There speaks a man who, if he is not a saint, still possesses himself in equanimity. He abides within the bounds of knowing what a man may do and what he may not do.

Macbeth has that same knowledge, but in his case the fences are shaky, and Lady Macbeth sets herself the task to make sure that her husband will break them down:

Glamis thou art, and Cawdor, and shalt be
What thou art promised; yet I do fear thy nature;

It is too full of the milk of human kindness
To catch the nearest way. Thou wouldst be great,
Art not without ambition, but without
The illness should attend it. What thou wouldst highly,
That wouldst thou holily; wouldst not play false,
And yet wouldst wrongly win. Thou'dst have, great Glamis,
That which cries, Thus thou must do, if thou have it;
And that which rather thou dost fear to do
Than wishest should be undone.

Her portrait of Macbeth is of a man bound not so much by virtue as by the wish to appear virtuous, and by a natural dislike of vice. He is all too ordinary, this great Macbeth. He doesn't want to cheat, but once the ill-gotten winnings are in, he does not give them back. He wants to be great, but he shies away from the vicious disease of ambition. That's his "nature," says Mrs. Macbeth, who then proceeds to tell us that she, for his sake, good and all too ordinary wife that she is, will unsex herself, begging the demons themselves, "murthering ministers," to take the milk of her breasts for gall and fill her up with cruelty.

Part of the tragedy of *Macbeth* is that the opportunity for greatness is presented to the man's ambition by a means that is "transgressive" all the way around—and I should mention that for Shakespeare, as it was for the ancient Romans, ambition is always a vice and betrays a deep moral disorder in the soul. It sets Lady Macbeth against the tenderness natural for her sex; she betrays this contradiction at several crucial moments in the play, such as when she says to the audience that she would have killed King Duncan herself, had he not resembled her father as he slept. It sets Macbeth against his own kinsman, the guest in his own home, his great benefactor, beloved of the Scots. There is no reason at all for the murder, says Macbeth:

I have no spur
To prick the sides of my intent, but only
Vaulting ambition, which o'erleaps itself
And falls on the other.

And it is "predicted" by those "sisters" of ambiguous sex, in words that are also ambiguous, seeming to promise what they retract. It is of the essence of the temptation that the prophecy be equivocal, unstable, misty, like the battlefield itself at the opening of the play. "So foul and fair a day I have not seen," says Macbeth.

What happens to Macbeth once he acts upon the suggestions? He cannot make the crooked straight by a royal decree. He cannot think what is wrong out of existence. We may freely choose to do what is right, or we may freely choose to do what is wrong, but we are not free to choose the consequences. I may drive my truck in reverse at fifty miles an hour; I am free to violate the structure of my truck. I am not free to do so without ruining its drive train. I am free to have my leg wrenched out of its socket. I am not free to walk without a limp afterwards. Macbeth may kill King Duncan. But as soon as he does so, he finds himself wrapped in the tangles of the evil; he is enslaved to it. "Things bad begun make strong themselves by ill," he says, attempting to justify hiring human wretches to assassinate Banquo and his young son. How strong? One evil "plucks on" another, until Macbeth is habituated to it, self-compelled. He was frightened by the cry of owls on the night he murdered Duncan. But on the night when his once-beloved wife, her mind deranged by evil and guilt and despair, takes her own life and her maids cry out in horror, Macbeth does not shiver:

I have almost forgot the taste of fears:
The time has been, my senses would have cooled
To hear a night-shriek, and my fell of hair

Would at a dismal treatise rouse and stir
As life were in't. I have supped full with horrors;
Direness, familiar to my slaughterous thoughts,
Cannot once start me.

That is not courage. There's no heart left in Macbeth, but an unnatural blood-pumping stone.

I often hear the canard that it is not the business of law to "impose" morality. People who say such a thing must doubtless mean "sexual morality," because even a passing thought reveals to us that imposing morality in one form or another is the principal thing that law does. All we have to do to see this is to enter a different arena. We cannot speak reasonably now about sex. All right, let us speak about honor. It wasn't so long ago, in the United States, that a man could challenge another to a duel if he believed that his honor or his wife's honor had been besmirched. "But that involves the loss of a human life!" cry the objectors, to which I reply, "Yes, and so does abortion," and also, "Kindly refrain from begging the question. So what if it does involve the loss of a human life?" Those who wished to justify the duel readily acknowledged the fact that men died by them; that was their intention, after all. They would also deny that dueling was the same as murder, since, in a duel, both parties consent. No one is compelled to fight. "Why should you impose your vision of morality upon us?" say the duelists.

The best answer is not, "Because we are in the majority." So were the Nazis for a while in Germany. So were the Aztecs when they drenched their temple with the blood of human sacrifice. The best answer is, "Because in fact you are *wrong* to duel, your code of honor is twisted, since it subjects the higher good of human life to the lesser good of respectability and face-saving." If the duelists wish, they may engage us in moral reasoning. What they may not do is to foreclose the whole issue by declaring a necessary libertarianism with regard to their favored behavior. Let them tell us why dueling is good and why allowing it makes for a better world; a sweeter world, a more stable community life, a world in which human life is held in high esteem. Let them argue for it on its merits.

The work of law is far more extensive and subtle than we usually suppose. When we forbid murder, we do not do so as a merely pragmatic act. We express by the law a moral understanding about human life. We teach ourselves and others that murder is more than illegal. It is *wrong*. We do not simply lock killers away to keep them from further killing. We *punish* them: we exact a penalty for the crime. That is why those who commit such serious crimes as murder are not prosecuted merely for having violated the rights of individuals. If one hired assassin murders another hired assassin, we are in one sense the better off for it; we have one fewer hired assassin on the loose. But the killer has violated the moral structure of the community. It isn't just that we can't set the precedent of letting an assassin go free if he kills another assassin. We must not think of these things in a simplistic and utilitarian way. The killer has committed an act of violence *against the people*, and it is *the people themselves*, not the family of the murdered man, who prosecute their case against the assassin.

The law, that which, as I've said, both confirms and invigorates our customs, doesn't just teach us as from without. It teaches us from within. A person who refrains from disobeying a just law is not the ideal citizen. He may, insofar as he regards just laws with indifference, hardly be called a citizen at all. He is compliant. But he has not taken to himself the moral vision that the law both implies and embodies. He does not "hear" the law in his conscience. He complies, as a slave might comply with his master's wishes, not willingly, but under duress. Or he complies, reckoning that it's to his advantage to do so, wrapped in his selfishness and never troubling to consider the common good. Such a man does not really obey. He does not really possess the virtue of justice. He hasn't made the just law an interior rule to himself, a habit.

When times are bad, when the country is convulsed in civil war, when looters are smashing windows in the streets, when the guardrails are down, such a person cannot be relied upon to do what is right. He is essentially lawless. He of all people needs the guardrails of both custom and law, if he is ever really to come to the full human flourishing that is impossible without virtue, which by its nature is demanding and difficult.

It's the art of the statesman to determine just *how* to embody the moral law in the civil law; what will be punished and how; what will be merely discouraged; what will be rewarded; what will be left to the ordinary and daily ministrations of people to manage without requiring a specific law on the books. Again, the question is not *whether* a moral vision will be embodied in the civil law, but which vision, and how.

We'll always need to strike a wise balance between punishment of severe crimes, discouragement and deterrence of lesser crimes, and tolerance of crimes which may be serious enough but whose punishment would embroil us in worse troubles still. We don't want to crucify the jaywalker. But we also don't want to roll out a carpet for the housebreaker. We may believe it would do more harm than good to try to outlaw all use of such drugs as marijuana. But we may still not want to allow pharmacies to sell LSD, and we may still want to fire the teacher who rolls joints in the lounge and laughs about it with his students. In determining what course of action to take against one wrong or another, we have more in mind than the welfare of the whole, or the welfare of those who may be hurt by people who engage in the wrong. We must consider the welfare of the wrongdoers also. We want them, first, to keep the wrong within modest bounds; then to abstain from the wrong; then to become truly healthy and take to their hearts what is right. We may, for example, decide to *tolerate* the use of marijuana, on the pragmatic grounds that its proscription embroils us in a constant struggle against organized crime. But if we really have the welfare of users in mind, we wouldn't want to stop there, even if we did decriminalize the thing. We would want them to abstain from the drug; then at last to adopt a healthy and sane way of life, breathing free, clean of the very temptation.

There's no reason to suppose that there's something special about sexual issues that would separate them from those involving money or testimonies in court or military duties or medicine or anything else in human affairs. On the contrary, as I've said, a people's customs and laws regarding sexual congress, marriage, and the family are deeply determinative of what sort of culture they will have; whether they will, for example, live in a world filled with children playing, or in an open sewer or a dirty alley, where children become precocious in wickedness, as cynical at age twelve as a thrice-divorced woman curdling her anger with gin and cigarettes. It is consistent to be a libertarian in matters of both money and sex; consistent, but quite insane. It is incoherent to be a libertarian in one and not in the other. The same moral law that forbids your neighbor from taking your lawn mower forbids him from taking your wife. The same moral law that forbids the odd old man down the road from aiming his car at your child to scare him forbids him from aiming his porn at your child to corrupt him.

So I am making the case that with regard to sodomy, as with regard to everything else in human life, we can reach a point after which tolerance becomes permission, and permission does harm to the very people who seem at first to enjoy the permissiveness. It denies them a good that they should have, and it encourages them to proceed in what hurts them first of all.

The best society for somebody inclined to violence is not revolutionary France. The best workplace for somebody inclined to avarice is not the New York Stock Exchange. The best city for a man who is attracted sexually to other men is not San Francisco or Seattle or Vancouver or Amsterdam. It may not be the Plymouth Colony, either, but that is another matter.

For I am not talking about cruel severity. If people understand that some folks are unfortunately attracted to members of their own sex, and if, while they neither seek to reveal it nor feel compelled to punish it, they make it known by custom that they do not approve of it, then the homosexual is provided with a merciful curb on his behavior. Both virtues and vices are habits, but they are habits that differ not simply in their objects but in their nature, their structure. The habits of virtue liberate. The brave man doesn't seem to be exerting any effort to stand up against the bully. The generous man doesn't seem to be struggling with himself as he welcomes his poor cousin into his home. Virtue is potent, effectual, manifold in its works. The virtuous husband is free to compliment the beauty of a woman without the suspicion crossing anybody's mind that he is up to something. Virtue is to the human soul as skill is to the artist. Perry Como sings apparently without effort. Rembrandt could make a pencil sketch in a few minutes that a lesser artist could only produce with cramped knuckles and sweat. Michelangelo spent a lot of time when he was a boy at the marble quarries in Carrara, and all that close experience of the quality of the stone, earned at first with patience and practice and error and much determined struggle, eventually set him free to "see" in a block of marble the David that nobody else could see in it.

But the habits of vice aren't like that. They don't invigorate; they deaden. They don't liberate; they compel. When we accustom ourselves to doing what is wrong—when we call the crooked straight and the warped smooth and the bizarre normal—we don't change the nature of our actions. We overlay our nature with a false nature, a parodic nature which must constantly cry out to be justified. We pick at the old unhealed wounds. We return to the scene of the crime. It isn't that Macbeth must, out of pragmatism, kill Banquo to secure his throne. It is that he has come to invite his evil impulses and deeds. He wants to do what he loathes to do, and wants it all the more because he loathes it. The duelist who shoots a man through the heart for insulting him may, we hope, repent of the great evil that he has done. But if he is thronged by people who slap him on the back for the good shot, who toast his courage, who hold him up as an exemplar of manhood, then even though he knows that they are wrong, what he has done may come to exercise a peculiar fascination for him. He sees the man bleeding out his life. He says, "Never have I felt more alive than I did at that moment." And he may then go and seek occasion for another duel. What at first struck him with horror becomes compulsive.

Pornography works in the same way. I recall the first time I ever saw a pornographic picture. There was a seedy little grocery store a few blocks from my house. My mother didn't like the man who owned it, so she never sent me there to get anything, but when I was ten years old I took up a newspaper route, and that store was on the street I worked. So I might go in there once in a while to pick up a carton of orange juice when I was thirsty. It was on one such occasion that a neighbor of mine, younger than I was, called me into the little room in back with a pool table. I was pretty skilled with the cue and the chalk. So I went in, and there on the wall, in plain sight of all the boys who would go back there to shoot pool, was a big humorous picture of a naked blonde, from the back, answering the door for an astonished caller.

I was mortified. I felt as you'd feel if you walked in on somebody you respected, doing something low and shameful.

My thought was, "How could a human being do a thing like that?" It was so unworthy of the woman, unworthy of the man, unworthy of the storekeeper. So I left the room, and my friend understood, too, that the picture wasn't right. But he was used to it. The next stage is to need it, and once that happens, the smutty picture I saw on the wall of the grocery store would hardly suffice. People who return to the scene of the crime of pornography will not be so easily satisfied. That's because what compels is not merely the object, but the very *wrongness of the object*. Mere garden sins bring boredom. We must rouse the spirit to more and more outrageous wrongs. I am speaking here not about sins of intemperance, such as eating too much or grouching at your children or being impatient with a slow student. I'm speaking about the wanton deviation into a territory clearly set aside as wrong in itself. It is the false excitement of the transgression that hooks us like the foolish fish we are.

The principle is borne out by all kinds of people who engage in sexual actions that are wrong not just by attendant circumstances, but in themselves and under any circumstances. Look for instance at the notorious Dan Savage, the gay advice columnist whose work is featured in arts newspapers across the country. His language is habitually violent and obscene. He seems to be filled with hatred against anybody who believes in anything less than what the furthest advanced of the sexual revolutionaries demand. It's a mark of our madness and irresponsibility that this fellow, who is deeply unbalanced, is invited to public schools to advise the students that being homosexual "gets better," thus encouraging them in the kinds of sexual experimentation that would land some of them at the same horrible place where he himself is standing. When, at one school, he began to rail against Jesus, some of the Christian students quietly got up and left the hall, whereupon he subjected them to a volley of ridicule, to the applause of some of their fellows in the audience. I cannot imagine for any reason subjecting young people to ridicule. But the self-contradiction seems to have escaped the notice of the promoters of Savage, who is pretending to go about fighting the bullies, when he himself is a bully, spoiled, hurt, angry, and vindictive, as even a passing acquaintance with his advice would show. Porn's all right for him, mutually agreed-upon cruelty, multiple partners, prostitution, whatever; everything is all right except what really is all right. Yet for all his wealth and fame, he hasn't gotten better at all.

He's not unique. He shows us why homosexuals seem to plunge further into the bizarre and self-destructive, precisely in those places where bigotry against them is slightest. For they themselves admit that they delight in being "transgressive," crossing the boundaries of what is decent or even mentionable. It follows that the nature of the transgressing behavior will depend upon where the society draws the line. If it draws the line rather close, the homosexual may rest content with merely crossing that line where it is. If, to be specific, it is unspeakable to suggest that a man will engage in a particular form of sexual release with another man, then the transgressor can do that, and let there be an end of it.

But if the line is drawn farther off, or not drawn at all, then the homosexual must go ever further for the same thrill of transgression. He must invent new methods, new combinations. Not content with merely inserting his organ of generation in the place of evacuation and uncleanness, he has to insert his fist there too—and we are subjected to the absurdity of school officials nodding in their superior wisdom as Mr. Savage explains to teenagers that you really can shape your fist so that it won't cause intense pain or tear the rectum or do a host of other things that he won't tell them about, because they involve diseases like hepatitis, and it's best to hide those things from teenagers who are apt to be squeamish about people sneezing on their lunch, let alone invading their intestines.

One of my close relatives is a specialist in infectious diseases, and she has told me that when she was an intern twenty years ago (and things are far worse now), they had to have long pornographic lessons in the unnatural things that people do with their reproductive organs; some of these were heterosexual; more were homosexual. Everyone has heard about AIDS, but that's just the most notorious of a wide array of diseases that afflict the homosexual man, including, for obvious reasons, diseases of the rectum, the colon, and the liver. When a man shows up at the clinic with any one of a number of these serious troubles, the first question the doctor has to ask is whether he has sexual relations with other men. But we won't tell that to our children, no, nor to men who may be tempted to cross that broken fence. I suspect it's because we understand that we're all at fault; we have all been compromised by the sexual revolution, and we all know that we can't be frank about what's wrong with the five men in the bathhouse, unless we will also be frank about what's wrong with the man living with his fifth wife, or the boy who is sleeping with his fifth girlfriend, or the woman who has aborted her fifth child. We're all implicated. Do homosexual men die earlier than men who smoke and drink too much? Yes, much earlier. But what should we care? It's their choice—and ours, too, to fornicate, divorce, flip the pages of the squalid magazine, and snuff out the lives of inconvenient babies. A poor charity indeed.

Tenth Argument

We Should Not Subordinate the Welfare of Children to the Sexual Predilections of Adults

WHEN I was growing up, I knew a boy who was raised by two women.

He was a year older than I was, and his backyard bordered on my backyard. We moved a couple of blocks away when I was eleven, but before that I saw him all the time, and even after that I saw him a lot, too. We were never friends. He didn't really have any friends, though he would sometimes play baseball or football with us. He was a decent player, not exceptional, but he was strong in the shoulders and the legs, and if he wanted to he could put a severe beating on anybody who made fun of him.

He did occasionally have to suffer taunting. Whenever his supper was ready, one of the women, a scrawny little lady with a turkey neck, would holler for him from the back door in a rising yodel-like call, turning his name into a ridiculous diminutive. We boys would sometimes mock him by imitating her. The other woman was a little inattentive and overprotective at once. So the kid—I'll call him Jimmy—didn't get to do much in the neighborhood. He was on a short leash. On the other hand, he got away with whatever he could. He had a foul mouth, even when he was only a five-year-old boy. One time my mother caught him doing something rotten and scolded him for it, for which he greeted her with a volley of dirty imprecations. She threw him out of the yard and told him that he would never step foot in it again until he learned his manners. So, as she tells the story many years later, he'd walk up to the invisible edge of his yard and ours, and stand there in the open and hurl at my mother every foul word he knew. She didn't make too big a fuss over it, because she understood that Jimmy already didn't have the best of lives.

Jimmy was, in short, a bully, but shy and angry too, as many bullies are. He was always fascinated with boyish things, like guns. He once shot my collie with a pellet gun. He also liked bicycles, cars, firecrackers, things that made noise, toys and not-toys that made things happen. In all these pastimes he was almost always alone. The two women spent most of their time either in the house or at work. The sturdier of the two would sometimes yell at him if he made too much noise, but generally his behavior ranged from surly compliance to contemptuous disregard. Yet for all that he rarely left the close vicinity of his backyard. When he did leave it, it was to traipse into the woods, alone.

He still lives in that house, I believe. He found a good woman to marry, and they have children. He became a policeman, as a lot of such kids do; he found a way to turn his aggressiveness to serve the common good. But he had a lonely and unhappy childhood. None of the other many children in the neighborhood would have wanted it.

The women stayed faithful to one another all their lives. Why should they not have? They were his widowed mother and his grandmother. A heart attack deprived Jimmy of a father while he was growing up, the father who could have taken him fishing, skeet shooting, hiking in the woods, or picking blueberries. His mother never crawled underneath a car, but his father might have, to teach him how they work. His mother never rode a bicycle, but his father might have, to take him on jaunts. There were a lot of sweet, ordinary things Jimmy missed out on, just because he didn't have a father. His mother wasn't to blame for it. But there it was. I doubt that Jimmy was ever comfortable around girls until he was well out of his teens. He's on his feet now, but there's no way he would wish for his children anything like what he suffered when he was a child.

In Jimmy's case, his missing his father did not land him on a list of statistics. He didn't drop out of school, he didn't use drugs, and he didn't find himself staring at the cinderblock walls of a jail cell. But we could hardly call his youth a rousing success. The heart of a human reality cannot be captured by numbers. What number can capture gray? What statistic can reveal the look in his eyes as he saw me and my cousins and my uncle playing touch football in the yard a hundred feet from his? And if the early death of his father was tragic, if it brought him years of sadness or loneliness or frustration, what are we to say about people who would *set out to deprive him of a father*? What would we say about people who would, in full control of the situation, see to it that a child would be conceived by a mother employed as an incubator, or begotten by a father employed as a stud bull, and then would shunt mother or father away to the outskirts of the child's life, or forget them altogether? Why is it a sad thing for a child, when one of his parents dies when he is little, perhaps even too little to remember, then to be raised by the survivor and, let's say he's lucky, a grandparent or an aunt or an uncle—somebody whose relationship to the surviving parent is close and matter-of-course and not prone to the storms of sexual passion—but not a downright wicked thing to force that sadness upon the child, all because of one's own sexual predilections?

And more than sadness. Let's say that Jimmy hadn't been raised by his mother and his grandmother. Let's say that Jimmy's mother had divorced his father and taken up with another woman. Jimmy will very soon know that this has happened. He must then be told one of two things, both of them devastating to his self-understanding as a boy. He must be told that his father was intolerable, so vicious, or so stupid, or so dull, or so anything else to be loathed, that his mother not only severed her ties with him, she washed her hands of the whole sex. Or he must be told that the father, although he wasn't so terrible, just could not in some mysterious way "satisfy" the mother, and so bad was this dissatisfaction that she had no choice but to compel her son to live without a father. The message to the child is clear enough. It's not just that the mother has rejected one man. She has rejected all men. Adults are wonderfully adept at weaving webs of self-deceit around themselves for protection. Children aren't. There are many things children don't see at all, because they don't yet have broad experience, but they aren't yet dulled by habit or by slogans or by a long history of compromising with the truth, so that what they do see, they see clearly. Jimmy would have seen this: that his sex was in itself bad. And this too: that there was nothing that his sex had to offer for the opposite sex. He wasn't for women, because they weren't for him. He'd be an alien in his own home. Of course, being a boy, he'd naturally desire to protect his best girl, his mother, from pain, and his mother would naturally desire him to do that too, regardless of her professed dismissal of the opposite sex. So he would be caught in the toils of self-contradiction. He'd have to play the man, to buck up, to protect his mother from feeling hurt; his love would instruct him never to cast her failure or her betrayal in her teeth; and he would derive absolutely no honor from a sacrifice no mere child should be required to make.

If we pretend that a man *can marry* another man, or a woman can marry another woman, we have consigned sex to irrelevance in a matter of plain biology. Then we can hardly consider it relevant in the far more complex but more subtle matter of anthropology. If a man can be the "wife" of another man, then we have to allow him to be the "mother" of a little girl. We have to pretend that sex does not matter for anything at all. We thus subject children, who are incapable of making our mental evasions, to the deprivation of a parent of their own sex or of the opposite sex, and to a world in which they can be given no clear guidance as to what they are as boys and girls. We become authors of confusion.

Allow me to draw out two implications here. They bear upon what we will have. I'll defer to the final chapter a picture of what we will lose. The first implication is this: we will have a culture whose moral structure is abusive to children.

For the moral structure of pedophilia is simply this: the welfare of children is subordinate to the sexual gratification of adults.

Jerry Sandusky, defensive coordinator for the football team at Penn State, established a charity called The Second Mile for mostly fatherless boys who were living in troubled homes. It's not clear that he did so initially to lure boys into a trap. But that's what eventually happened, according to the testimony of the men who recalled with shame and disgust their initiation into sodomy.

Raymond Lahey, Catholic bishop of Antigonish, was apprehended in the Ottawa airport and his computer files scanned. They contained nude pictures of boys. Lahey resigned in disgrace. The Canadian press tried hard to conceal the sex of the children, and suppressed any report about the exotic destinations to which the bishop commonly flew. One isn't to inquire too closely into travel agencies that do a hopping business flying men to Thailand, which teems with boy prostitutes. And girl prostitutes, too; Thailand is a favorite sweating-off ground for Korean businessmen.

We should be thankful that the Laheys and Sanduskys are still considered monstrous. But that condemnation now rests on sentiment and not on moral reasoning. Nobody can simultaneously explain *why* their actions were so vile, and uphold the first commandment of the sexual revolution: fulfill thy desires. For there's a difference between what is merely wrong, like taking an apple from a fruit stand, and what is wrong and despicable because it suggests a certain baseness, like taking an apple from a child's lunch, and what is wrong and *heinous*, because the wickedness involves a peculiar cruelty or malignity or corruption. What these men did was *heinous*. We know this. But why?

It may be argued that the boys were too young to give genuine consent. They were dupes. That may be true of the boys in Pennsylvania, but it cannot be true of the hardened street children in Bangkok. But the horror, the disgust, is out of all proportion to a memory of being duped. If somebody tricks a boy into giving him fifty dollars for a lump of fool's gold, the grown man will look back on the incident with irritation and contempt for the trickster, but not horror. That trickery is despicable, but not heinous. The shame of Sandusky's victims rose not from the trickery, but from the corrupt act itself into which they were tricked.

Besides, the fact that a child cannot give consent is not in itself morally decisive. We compel children to do plenty of things for their own good—or for what we say is good. A public school teacher in Toronto has written a set of lessons requiring young children to imagine wearing clothes appropriate for the opposite sex. He's been congratulated, not by the wary parents, but by a school board that insists that teachers are "co-parents."

What he's doing, of course, is subjecting naïve children to an exercise that promotes his own sexual aims. If the man down the street did the same thing, we'd consider him a dangerous creep, and we'd call the police. The difference between the teacher and the creep is that the creep's capacity to do harm is far more limited. The teacher has a powerful institution at his back, and gets to fiddle with the sexual imaginations of twenty-five children at a time.

No, it isn't *how* Sandusky and Lahey did what they did, or under what circumstances, that explains the disgust. It's *what* they did—but nobody wants to acknowledge that, because nobody wants to acknowledge the reality of what it means to be a boy or a girl.

The reason for that reluctance becomes clear, if we keep in mind the moral structure of pedophilia. As I've said, sexual gratification is trumps. Thank goodness that, for now, there aren't many men who are sexually attracted to youngsters (though, if we take them at their word, most homosexual men are indeed attracted to adolescent males). In that single case, we raise the banner for the children. But in no other case.

If we altered the question and asked not how many people have done sexually abusive things with children, but how many people *have done sexual things that redounded to the suffering of children*, then we might confess that the only thing that separates millions of people from Jerry Sandusky is inclination. Everything that was once considered a sexual evil and that is now winked at or cheered, everything without exception, has served to hurt children, and badly.

We may point here to each of the evils of the sexual revolution that I've already touched upon. Unless it's necessary to remove oneself and one's children from physical danger and moral corruption, the old wisdom regarding divorce should hold, if children themselves have anything to say about it.

Parents will say, "My children can never be happy unless I am happy," but they should not lay that narcissistic unction to their souls. Children need parents who love them, not parents who are contented; they are too young to be asked to lay down their lives for someone else. It's not the job of the child to suffer for the parent, but the job of the parent to endure, to make the best of a poor situation, to swallow his pride, to bend her knees, for the sake of the child. I have heard from people at the extreme limit of old age, who still quaver in the voice when they speak about what their divorcing parents did to them—hustling them from one half of a home to another half, enlisting them as confidants one against the other, sometimes holding the hammer silently over the head of the child, who may just find himself a lot less often with the parent he loves, if he does not do exactly what the hammer-holder wants. Children must grow up at age ten, so that their parents don't have to.

We might point to births out of wedlock. The child has a right to enter more than a little nursery decorated with presents from a baby shower. He should enter a human world, a story, a people. He should be born of a mother and father among uncles and aunts and cousins and grandparents, stretching into the distant past, with all their interrelated histories, with his very *being* reflected in all those mirrors of relation, not to mention his eyes and his hair, the talents in his fingers and the cleverness in his mind. This *belonging* to a big and dependable world can be secured only in the context of the *permanent* love of his mother and father, declared by a vow before the community and before the One in whom there is no shadow of alteration.

Planned Parenthood (Planned Predators would perhaps be more apt) have long declared, with crocodilian tears, that every child should be a *wanted child*, predicating the child's value upon the lusts of the parents, rather than valuing the parents' actions according to the being and the beauty of a child. Perhaps an honorary statue of Jerry Sandusky should stand outside every Planned Parenthood abortuary. Sandusky certainly *wanted* children. If not Sandusky, then Alfred Kinsey, pervert and fraud, who conned the useful, broadminded, American morality-stretchers while hiring criminals to engage in sexual abuse of infants and small children. The dry sewer called Hollywood a few years ago celebrated the professor in a feature film. If devils are allowed reading material, maybe Alfred Kinsey enjoys the odd moment or two, smiling as he peruses our sex education curricula.

Is that unfair? Some people want to have their sexual flings, but are discreet enough to try to keep children away from them; not that they ever succeed entirely, but at least their hypocrisy pays vice's tribute to virtue. But Planned Parenthood does not believe in that tribute. There are pedophiles of the body, and pedophiles of the soul. Planned Parenthood happily enlists the latter among their troops.

Most parents grow reticent when the time comes to tell their children about sex. That reticence is right and natural, as is the quiet of a man's voice as he brings his son to a holy place, the grave of his grandfather who died in the war, or the little old house where his grandmother was born. Sex is not about the mechanics. The parent must tell the child about the love that brought him into being; and therefore sex is about the past and the present and the future, and about all those who share in the great family network of begetting and of love.

Then in comes Planned Parenthood, with a cadre of—what shall we call them? What would we call them if they had no "credentials," no initials after their names? What would we call the old man down the street, wheezing and giggling, who likes to show little kids pictures of people masturbating? So then, along comes PP with their creeps, lubriciously introducing children to the delights of meaningless sex, with cartoons of talking penises and vaginas, of a girl bending over with a mirror to inspect her anus, or a boy in his bedroom abusing himself.

One wonders how Sandusky managed to do what he did for so long, without getting caught by parents. Well, the abuser separates the child from the parents. "This is our secret," says the creep. "Don't tell your parents," sibilates the lizard. "They won't understand." "Your parents haven't treated you right," hisses the snake. "Your parents are old-fashioned. Your parents are selfish. Your parents have their own agenda. You don't have to submit to your parents. You can be your own person," wheedles the weasel, meaning: *submit to me.*

That is the same strategy that the credentialed spiritual pederasts use. Mother and father are the enemy. Mother and father are kept in the dark. Mother and father are too benighted to know what's best. Mother and father—even such sporadically responsible mothers and fathers as our generation has produced—wouldn't know about how happy it is to be sexually free. "We's the ones wot knows is best, ain't we?" says the scholastic predator, flipping the well-thumbed page and pointing out the next cartoon. "Thinkee can do that there, hmm?"

One begins to wonder whether it is not the harm done to the child that counts, in our world of advertising-as-truth, but the style with which it is done, or the class to which the child-destroyer belongs. It's hard for those who don't think about the essences of things to judge actions and not actors. So the soggy-jowled, sweaty, old football coach Sandusky pins a boy to the wrestling mat and has his way, and he is justly condemned for it, but the little girl-loving Jerry Savile, darling of the BBC, flaunts his immorality for years, to the knowing jests of many an unreporting reporter. So Kermit Gosnell, a man with the morals of Josef Mengele but without the same surgical skills, is nonplussed to learn that many a reliable immoralist expresses disgust at his having turned abortion into more than a hand-over-fist moneymaker: a hobby, with a delightful trove of preserved parts, cut from their owners to the jaunty percussion of the scissors. What, after all, is he *doing* to those babies that differs in more than style from what the prim, waspish, feminist doctor is doing uptown in Rittenhouse Square? He laughs while he works, and she dons the serious mien of a soldier in the army of Equality, doing what she must, and making money for it. Mustn't muzzle that ox as she treads out the corn.

And the welfare case who, at her wits' end, takes a whip to the boy who can throw her to the floor, she is led off to family court, she with the tobacco stains on her fingers and the voice ground down into tenor. But the sophisticated "single mother," with her degree in Women's Studies from Wellesley, living in the high-rent belt around Boston, dresses her daughter up as a neuter, and turns a cold shoulder when the child begs to be treated like an ordinary girl. No time in jail for her; rather a date for the *savante nouvelle* to lecture at the local library, one week after her friend lectures on the cruelty of treating dogs as if they were not dogs, and one week before her other friend lectures on gluten-free wheat and yolkless eggs.

John Williamson, self-professed swinger, the proprietor of a massive nudist and adultery farm, receives from the national presses an obituary worthy of a great artist or inventor, and no one pauses to ask how many children's lives were snuffed out or made miserable by the perversions of their elders; but the former Pope Benedict, the gentle-spoken and staid professor of a morality that was not so long ago taken for granted by nearly everyone, could only wish to be treated with dull neutrality, or even respectful enmity.

But what here is new? Our society has been corrupting childhood for a long time, under the pretense of good hygiene, freedom of the press, academic freedom for schoolteachers, and personal fulfillment.

Why have we forgotten that it is crucial to our emotional and intellectual development that sexual feelings be latent during childhood? Why does any knowledge of the many thousands of years of development of the human race vanish from our minds just when it comes to the sexes? A male dog begins to raise his leg well before his first year is over. He is quickly ready to mate. Why isn't it so with human beings? Why does it take us so many years to grow to adulthood? Why, for those twelve to fourteen years (and, before our sugar-laden diet of processed foods laced with growth hormones, it used to be longer than that), are we children? Why do the boy's muscles thicken then, and his bones lengthen, and his voice deepen, and his chin sprout hair? Why not sooner? What is the advantage for so protracted a period of sexual latency?

It frees the time for what is then more important: learning. In the first instance, the boy learns to be a boy and then a man, so that afterwards he can marry; and the girl learns to be a girl and then a woman. But also the boys and girls are learning about the world around them, a world of duties and responsibilities. This social learning is short-circuited by a forced precocity in matters of sex. Other forms of learning are short-circuited, too. The boy who at age fifteen is not interested in girls may well be forging his way through calculus, or learning to take cars apart and rebuild them from scratch. The girl who at fifteen is not interested in boys may be devouring the novels of Dickens. Since, given the many years we expect our children to be in school and then college, most will not marry until long after puberty, why on earth would we want to hurry the onset of the troubles? Would we of all people not want instead that our children should not even think seriously about the opposite sex until well into their teenage years, at the earliest?

But if homosexual "marriage" is accepted, there can be no such wise deferral. We will be visiting a crisis of identity upon every child in our society. That in fact is the intention of many homosexual activists, whose revenge upon the children who were once cruel or indifferent to them is to afflict other children with doubts, to make them endure the questions they themselves endured. All of this is done under the guise of charity for the homosexual teenager; but the true charity would refrain from plunging children into the trouble in the first place, and would instead offer an unambiguous expectation of heterosexuality. That would give many pubescent teens the wherewithal to shrug off the random doubt, rather than causing it to grow into a prognosis. But given the latency of sexual feelings during childhood, no child will be able to say with confidence, "I am a heterosexual"—how could the child even know what that means? He has no clear feelings to which the statement corresponds. In the meantime, what for boys and girls are wholly natural attractions to members of the same sex, in the years when they are forging their identities as boys and girls, will now be shaded with the suspicion of homosexuality—as if the boys and girls could really know what that meant, either!

There is no gainsaying it. If homosexual "marriage" is condoned, then of course kissing, holding hands, celebrating anniversaries, talking about your first date, and all the rest must be condoned. Children in Massachusetts must be subjected to the propaganda, because, says the man in charge, same-sex "marriage" is legal in the state—impossible biologically, but legal; so children will be compelled to participate in the confusion. If a teacher can casually mention where he met his wife, then the homosexual teacher can casually mention where he met his husband. Need I mention that logic compels us to travel to the end of this mistaken road? Why should not the bisexual mention to his third graders where he met his wife and then, after he divorced her, where he met his husband?

And at that we still haven't descended to the depth of the confusion. We're now told that we must celebrate the "transgendered," which refers not to people who have mutilated themselves to pretend to belong to the opposite sex, but to people who believe they are "really" women in men's bodies or men in women's bodies. Now this warrants some clear thinking. If I say that I am Napoleon, you will call for the psychiatrists and the men in white coats. That is because I am not Napoleon. My mind is not in concord with reality. But at least Napoleon did in fact exist. There might be method to my madness. I might be walking back and forth in my cell on Saint Helena, muttering, "It was all the fault of that Talleyrand!" I might be writing love letters to Josephine while the orderly brings in the bouillabaisse.

But what kind of madness is it if I say, simultaneously, "I am Napoleon," and "Napoleon does not exist"? That's not just confusion. It is confusion within confusion. And that is exactly the position of the "transgendered." We are to believe that, for the sake of children growing up in a sane and healthy way, it does not matter whether they have both a mother and a father, a parent of their own sex and of the opposite sex. It doesn't matter, we say, because sex doesn't matter. Sex is just a minor affair of plumbing. It's irrelevant, say the feminists. Its existence is superficial. But if that is the case, what can it possibly mean to say, "I am *really* a woman in a man's body"? It would be more sensible to say, "I am *really* a unicorn in a man's body," since the madman might imagine a unicorn with a characteristic unicorn nature; but these mad people have denied that there is any such thing as a woman's nature.

You can't have it both ways. You can't say that sex is irrelevant where it most obviously is determinative—as in marriage—adding to it that sex is *only* about our little naughty things, and at the same time say that you *must be* a man in a woman's body or a woman in a man's body. You can't insist upon crossing a bridge whose existence you have denied. The same goes for homosexual attraction. To what, after all, is the homosexual man attracted? If it is only a little tool, it seems absurd to convulse an entire culture over that. What would be the great sacrifice, then, if we asked the man in question to direct his attention to this other little thing over there, the one belonging to the lady? No, the very existence of men compulsively attracted to other men testifies to one thing most clearly—that *there are such things as men*, not just human beings with minor differences in the nether region. But if that is true, then the whole premise of feminism, which thrives in a symbiotic relationship with the sexual revolution, fails. We can't say at once, "The sex of a child's 'parents' doesn't matter," and then say that the sex of the person with whom the adult shares a bed matters so much that he or she can't possibly conform his or her ways to nature. The boy doesn't need a father, because sex doesn't matter; but his mother needs a "wife" and can't possibly be expected to take a man, because in this case sex matters more than everything else in the world.

Get used to it, kid. By the way, have you seen this new video game?

Eleventh Argument

We Should Not Give Godlike Powers to the State

W INSTON Smith has been imprisoned in the dungeons of the Ministry of Love. His corrector and tormentor, O'Brien, stands before him, holding out his hand with two fingers extended.

"How many fingers do you see, Smith?" O'Brien asks.

"Two," says Smith. He is exhausted, mind and body. He has been subjected to drug-induced madness, evil dreams of things that horrify him, like swarms of rats. He is trying to retain his now feeble hold upon sanity. But two is the wrong answer. After a long while, just to win some reprieve from the torment, Smith gives O'Brien the answer he desires.

"Three," says Smith.

"That is not sufficient," says O'Brien. "You are saying that, but you don't believe it. You must learn to train your mind to see what we require you to see. How many fingers am I holding out?" And after many sessions of educational correctness and torment, Smith brings himself to the position in which he can execute the necessary mental gymnastics. He finds a way to say, shutting his mind away from reality, that he does indeed see three fingers.

Many opponents of same-sex pseudogamy argue that the pretense that a man *can marry* another man will involve restrictions on the religious freedom of those who disagree. I don't believe there's much to dispute here. One side says that same sex-marriage will restrict religious liberty, and believes that that would be disgraceful and unjust; the other side says the same, and believes it is high time, and that the restrictions should have been laid down long ago. So when Fred Henry, the moderate liberal Catholic bishop of Edmonton, says that there is something intrinsically disordered about same-sex pseudogamous relations, he is dragged before a Canadian *human rights tribunal*, without anyone sensing the irony (one suspects that the leaders of George Orwell's Oceania at least indulged in a little mordant irony when they named their center of torment the Ministry of Love). Or when the Knights of Columbus find out that a gay couple has signed a lease for their hall to celebrate their pseudo-nuptials, and the chief retracts the invitation and offers to help the couple find another acceptable hall, the Knights are dragged into court. The same with the widow who ekes out her living by baking wedding cakes. And the parents in Massachusetts who don't want their children to be exposed to homosexual propaganda in the schools. And the Catholic adoption agency in Massachusetts that had to shut down rather than violate their morals, as the state demanded they do, placing children in pseudogamous households.

And the Boy Scouts... To see how upside down we are—how utterly insane—all one has to do is to consider how that once proud and noble organization, the Scouts, who did so much that was good for boys of all creeds and races, has been so reviled. In Philadelphia, they were driven from the headquarters which they themselves built at the city's request and then donated back to the city, all because they still retained the common sense notion that it is not healthy for still immature boys to be camping out with boys who declare that they are sexually aroused by boys.

Let's return to the Ministry of Love. Let's assume that, while there aren't many saints among us, there are not usually many madmen, either. There are not many people who will naturally say that they see three fingers when there are only two. There are not many people who will naturally say that a woman *can marry* another woman, when the obvious biology shows us otherwise. Go to any tribe in the world where the concerted harassment of government and mass media has not penetrated, and suggest to an ordinary woman with a little child hanging on her back that a woman *can marry* another woman, and, once she gathers that you are serious, she will fall to laughing so hard she will have to put the child down, and then, directing your attention to the dog marking his yard, or the bull strutting in the field, she'll tell you that there's something obvious you are missing—but perhaps there are women in the city who have those? And then she will break out into new peals of laughter, and will call her neighbors to join in the fun.

Mass madness, if it's going to last more than a week or two, requires mass media or mass government or the synergistic efforts of both. It isn't just that the pretense that a man can marry a man will put religious believers at a disadvantage. It's that it must set that ordinary tribeswoman in its sights, regardless of her religion. It's not just her faith she must renounce. She must renounce her common sense. She must not be allowed even to think that the pretense is insane. She must be re-educated to believe that two fingers are three fingers, or that the sun rises in the west, or that the child in her womb is really a rock, or that excrement is nutritious, or anything else that no sensible person would ever come to discover on her own.

And now come the embarrassingly flimsy objections. They can be organized into two categories. The first concerns improper restrictions upon marriage made by people in the past. The second concerns the State's role in regulating marriage.

Common sense, we are told, caused white people in the American South to pass anti-miscegenation laws, making it illegal for blacks and whites to intermarry. The desire for gay couples to marry is supposedly just like the desire of John Campanella, an immigrant from Sicily, to marry his sweetheart Ida, an African-American. They wouldn't have been allowed to do that in some of the southern states, but they lived in Pennsylvania, they did marry, and Ida gave birth to a son, Roy, who became a Hall of Fame catcher for the Dodgers. But as soon as we put it this way we see that the analogy doesn't hold. Of course John Campanella *could marry* Ida—they were a man and a woman! Nobody disputed that. The racists in the South did not dispute that. They did not deny the capacity of John and Ida to marry one another. They did not deny that John and Ida Campanella were in fact married, just as any man and woman would be. *They wanted to keep such marriages from happening.*

Nor is it fair to say that it was a matter of common sense. It was something pretty peculiar to America and the South, during the years of black slavery and its aftermath. The rest of human history doesn't bear it out. Yes, it's easy to find people of certain places, social classes, and times who do not want their daughter to marry the doctor from Parthia or the launderer from the Subura, but that involves whom you are going to marry and not what marriage itself is. Look at Central and South America and the Philippines—the places settled by the supposedly all-evil Spanish Catholics. What do we see? From the very start, we find all kinds of intermarrying between the Spaniards (and the Portuguese, too) and the natives, and not the peculiar and unhealthy preoccupation with race that has beset the United States. The same thing can be said about the French and their marriages with natives in North America;

that was quite common. Sacagawea, the Shoshone woman who helped Lewis and Clark find their way to the Pacific Ocean, was married to a French fur trader who accompanied the expedition also. Nobody doubted that they were married. Nobody doubted that they *could marry*. That is what men and women have always done. Saint Augustine was the son of Patricius and Monica, both natives to North Africa. Patricius is a Roman name, but that doesn't prove he was of Roman blood; men took Roman names regardless of their race or ethnicity. Monica was an African name, probably Semitic. We have no idea what was Augustine's "race," because nobody thought it was important enough to mention. So it's we who have suffered an unhealthy and unjust preoccupation with race—and in the mad matter of a man's supposedly being able to marry another man, we modern westerners are the oddballs, too.

In short, it is one thing to say that we should of course allow any man to marry any woman, regardless of money or class or race, so long as they are beyond a certain degree of consanguinity; it is another thing entirely for us to pretend that we can define marriage itself out of existence, pretending that it is not what it is—that two fingers are three and marriage is just close friendship with sex and a vague commitment to persistence, though not permanence.

And that answers the second category of objections—that it is not the State's role to regulate marriage—too. A people's laws and customs certainly ought to bear upon marriage, which may be their most important object. A society's long-held stance, set down in law, involves an understanding of what makes for healthy marriages, or happy marriages, or successful families, or other things pertaining to the common good. So we may say that a boy under the age of eighteen cannot marry without his parents' consent; that is because we have the good of marriage itself in mind, and the circumstances peculiar to someone so young. Or we may have a custom requiring the woman's father to offer a dowry with her in marriage; again that is because we have the good of marriage itself in mind, and the circumstances peculiar to a woman leaving one home and setting herself up in another. We may forbid divorce, or allow it under certain rare conditions, or make it as common as weeds, as we do now. But in none of these cases do we come near to touching the essence of marriage. We know from the first what marriage *is*: our laws and customs, if they are wise and just, will promote it, protect it, and foster it. The reality, though, is already there, to promote, protect, and foster; or to demote, endanger, and starve.

"But so what if the State does let Jim and Arthur pretend that they're married? What harm can that do?" I've spent this whole book touching upon the harms, and the harm that the sexual revolution has already done. Let me now add some more, as regards the State and the citizen.

People suppose that a Constitution, well observed, is all you need to prevent the State from arrogating to itself a godlike power to direct and manage all things for all people. The history of the last hundred years should put that daydream to rest; we are in a time when "interstate commerce" doesn't have to involve two states and doesn't have to be commercial, and when freedom of speech means license to sell dirty pictures, but *not* the freedom in public schools to say certain things about our polity, about morals, or about religion. In any case, the supposition isn't true and never could be true. People will always find ways around the constitutions that limit them; just as clever and mercurial lawyers have been able to turn our Constitution, a blueprint for intergovernmental relations which was supposed to limit the federal government, into a cultural creed for bludgeoning ordinary people and their folkways into submission to their betters. But a Constitution must always be somewhat distant and artificial. What really keeps the State in check are other zones of *authority*, recognized as natural, with prescriptive rights and duties and areas of interest.

It is not the State that defines what marriage is; nature has done that. It is not the State that determines the good of the family; nature has done that, too. It is not even the State that creates the village or the parish. Households have done that. Before there was ever a gross national product, there was *economy*, the law of the good of the *oikos*, the household. The ancient Greeks, who bequeathed to us both the term and the reality of democracy, understood that the individual as such was something of an abstraction. You belonged to a family, a household, a clan—and then, after the reforms of Cleisthenes, a *deme*, one of the political units of ancient Athens. Cleisthenes saw that it was necessary to redirect some of his countrymen's allegiance from the family to the greater city; and the struggle between those who favored the city and those who favored the family pretty much describes Athenian politics for the hundred years of its democracy. The republican Romans were better able to build the civic reality upon the reality of the family, and so their "public thing," their republic, lasted a lot longer than did democratic Athens.

It's not true that it's a sign of health when a thing keeps growing and growing. Cancers keep growing and growing; that is why cancers kill. *The growth of flesh is but a blister*, says the poet Herbert; *Childhood is health*. The healthy lung does not try to do the work of the stomach. A healthy State does what it is supposed to do, and does it reasonably well, and leaves to other political entities the work that they are supposed to do, including those political entities that are natural—the family foremost among them. But totalitarian regimes since Plato penned his *Republic* (and it's never been clear to me just how seriously Plato intended that exercise in totalism) have always been aimed against the family, and for good reason. The family is the single greatest bastion against the power of the State. That's not because of "individual" rights. It's because the family claims precedence in being and in nature. It is itself a society anterior to the greater society. It has its own just rules, its aims, its claims to obedience from its members, its promises, its duties, its power. In any land where there are strong, self-sustaining, culture-making, community-building families, the State, which may be a lot bigger but which is secondary in its nature, meets the hand of a lord who says, "Thus far you may go, and no farther." And this is, of course, why ambitious statists seek to co-opt the family, to regulate it from above and invade it from within. The State is a jealous god.

What the State essentially does, when it requires us to be parties to the lie that a man *can marry* a man, is to deny the anterior reality of marriage itself. It says, "Marriage is what we say it shall be," and that implies, "Families are what we say they are," and that implies, "There are no zones of natural author-ity outside the supervision and regulation and management of the State." We've given up on the foolish notion of the Divine Right of Kings, dreamed up by totalizing monarchs of the late Renaissance. Now we have the Divine Right of Bureaucratic States. The old kings used to make common cause with smaller zones of authority, guilds and towns, for example, in order to check the ambitions of the noblemen. The new kings have oblit-erated those smaller zones of authority in principle, and seek to do so in reality also. That is in large part what public schools are now for; the education of children *against the authority and direction of their own parents.*

I know there are libertarians who believe that the State should "get out of the marriage business entirely," but they are living in the dreamland made possible by the very same all-intrusive, bureaucratic, technocratic State they deplore. The growth of the State does not depend upon the obliteration of the individual, so much as it does upon the obliteration of nature and those natural communities that make for genuine citizenship in the first place. The metastatic State can make common cause with the individualism of licentiousness—with the sexual revolution—because they share the same enemies: the family, the neighborhood, the parish. The State profits from the chaos wrought by the destruction of the family, just as the totalitarian first destroys an economy and then declares that he's the only one who can restore order. The Nazis and the Communists marched arm in arm against the Social Democrats in the Weimar Republic, not because their enemies were wrong and were doing things harmful to the German economy. They wanted that economy to fail. They wanted chaos to erupt. Hitler wanted the chaos for his brand of total-itarianism, and the Communists wanted it for theirs. In the same way, it is quite true that American statists would not want to see more and more young men and women getting married, having a lot of children, staying married, taking care of their children on their own, and some of them even schooling their children on their own. That would severely cramp the ambi-tions of statists.

The lesson is simple. If you want true liberty and not just a paper pass—if you want actually to be able to walk down a back street at night without fear; if you want a real voice in what goes on in the school around the corner—then you want to bolster the family against the State. But you cannot do that if you grant to the State the godlike power to determine what a family or a marriage is in the first place.

And then there are the children. When a man and woman marry and do the thing that men and women do, they naturally have children. Nobody has to define what a father and a mother are. We know what they are. And nobody has to define what a child is. We know that, too.

But the relations between a man and a man or a woman and a woman are necessarily barren. The man is not going to beget a child by sowing his seed in the sewage area of another man; things don't work that way. The woman is not going to conceive a child by having another woman insert a piece of plastic in her; plastic doesn't work. So when we declare that they have a "right" to do what they cannot possibly do, when we declare that two fingers are three, then we automatically have declared that a child does not need either a mother or a father, and that the man-man desert or the woman-woman desert should be fruitful even though (by nature and not by accident) it could never be. That means we will have to *make* children for them, by unnatural and impersonal means; a womb for rent, sperm for sale, or manufacture in a laboratory.

It is the inevitable continuation of the Lonely Revolution, this alienation. We begin by severing sexual intercourse from its rightful home in marriage. We then find that we have severed it also from its natural connection to childbearing. And we have severed the natural love that men and women, in their interdependence, should bear to one another. And we sever husbands and wives in divorce, and "husbands" and "wives" in "divorce" that never makes it to the statistics because they never bothered to have a wedding to begin with. And we sever child from parent and brother from sister. Now we sever the conception of a child from the act of love that begets and conceives. And that means that, more than ever, the child will come to be seen as the product of the will-to-power of the parents. They want what they want, and will go to extraordinary means to get it.

It is impossible to avoid. If you accept that a woman and a woman may cobble together the DNA to "make" a child that will fulfill them, you have already crossed a fearful divide. The man and woman who make love are doing the natural thing by which they themselves were brought into being. It is right, it is ordinary, and if their hearts are in the right place, they will accept whatever child may be born from this love. But people—heterosexuals too—who demand the "right" to manufacture a child are already seeing the child as a thing, a commodity, an accessory to their lifestyles, like a human time-share for a condominium in Cancun. They then begin, as we are seeing before us even now, to demand the "best" quality, exactly as if they were shopping for a car. Perish the thought that the child from the child factory might have Down Syndrome—that child, via prenatal screening, will be labeled a Factory Reject and tossed in the garbage. "To the dump with it," say the parents and the manufacturers—well, they don't say that, because that smacks of the lower classes; but that is the reality.

There's nothing then preventing us from all the manifold evils of eugenics—cloning, screening out "defectives," mingling genes from various "parents," even engineering new breeds of the human race, as if we were no different from cows or goats. That too is being pushed by the self-styled "transhumanists." And who is going to oversee the manufacture? Why, the State, of course. The State will oversee it. Who else? We couldn't really have any old madman commissioning the cloning of himself twenty times over, could we? No, we would have to place reasonable limits on that sort of thing. The State will regulate what kinds of people come into the world, and their numbers. At which point, as C. S. Lewis observed, the next generation is completely subject to the control and determination of the previous generation. It isn't just that the elder will teach the younger. That is natural and everywhere to be found in human societies, and it is what helps to bind the generations together. It is that the elder will *create* the younger, for its own purposes. Man's hunger to dominate nature devours him first of all. In the very moment of what appears to be his greatest triumph, he becomes an abject slave. He cannot treat the embryo as a product, a thing for sale, a commodity to be priced according to the probabilities that it will exhibit musical talent or a genius for physics or broad shoulders for football, without *ipso facto* demoting himself to the same status.

I do not want to live in a world planned by eugenicists. I think that the cloning of a human being ought to be considered the most serious of crimes, more serious than murder, because it puts humanity itself to death. But I know that pseudogamous couples hail the coming of that further foray into the unnatural. They favor the manufacture of children. They cheer at the prospect of cloning. There's a lot of money to be made by the manufacturers, and a lot of power to be gleaned by the State. And the State, in arrogating to itself the authority to determine what a family is, and what kinds of children we may produce, will have resumed its atavistic status as a god, its priest-politicians our masters, and ordinary people dwelling in the shadow of the pyramids, little better than slaves.

Twelfth Argument

The Beauty of the Country of Marriage

THE disciples were engaging in the ancient pastime of sinful and selfish man. They were arguing over which of them would be the greatest in the Kingdom of Heaven.

Jesus asked them what the quarrel was about. Doubtless he wanted them to utter the words themselves, half abashed even before he would rebuke them. Then Jesus did something that changed the orientation of the world. For the world lusts for power and wealth and glory and the pleasures of the body. The world never learns. The world should heed the words that the loyal Fool spoke to King Lear: *Thou shouldst not have been old till thou hadst been wise.*

So Jesus took a little child and set him in their midst. Then He said, "Truly I tell you, unless you become as one of these little ones, you shall not enter the Kingdom of Heaven."

He might have said, too, that if anything like a sweet and lovely life is to be had on earth, any foretaste of the promised Kingdom, it too can only be accepted as by a child. It cannot be manufactured in a Joy Factory, it cannot be lavished upon the people by politicians hammering out a Beauty Bill, it cannot be distilled by scientists seeking the Essence of Grace. We cannot have a good country unless we are good people, and we cannot be good people unless we recover the humility and the innocence of the child.

The land of marriage is the land that is not only fit for the child. It is inhabited by the childlike. It is built and fostered, swept clean and festooned with streamers on the holidays, kept warm and hospitable, by people whose lives recall the words of Jesus, who welcome children into their midst because they too strive to be like children.

In Fra Angelico's painting of the Final Judgment, there's a good lot of action going on, with saints pressing forward as they look upon Christ enthroned, and the wicked being hauled down to Hell, and the lids of tombs lying scattered across the broad central avenue. But on one side there's a garden full of flowers, and small children are dancing with angels in a ring, as if Judgment Day were a day like any other under the sun. The Land of Marriage is like that.

In the Land of Marriage there are many weddings, and the brides and the bridegrooms are young and full of life. What matter if they don't have a lot of money? Don't be fooled by his still boyish voice, or by the girlish way she plays with her curls. He is all for her and she is all for him, and they know how to do the simple things for one another that make life more than possible. They make life good. All her life she has been prepared for this day, when she would give herself over entirely to one man, and all his life he has been prepared for this day, when he would give himself over entirely to one woman. In the Land of Marriage, you don't need sureties from the future. What adventure can there be if you must always have all the odds reckoned up? Who wishes to sail to an unknown island with a calculator? In this Land, the bride and groom stand tall and noble because they do not know what will happen, and they would not want things any other way. No true child would.

In the Land of Marriage, men and women cherish one another, delight in one another's strengths, laugh at one another's foibles, and bear with one another's weaknesses. Gratitude, that virtue so close both to greatness of heart and to the wonder of a child, is the order of the day. When the women look upon men digging ore out of the heart of a mountain, or laying roads, or bending their strong arms and large hands to shave the marble one grain of dust at a time, and give it the smoothness of a baby's cheek, they are grateful, not envious. It pleases them to see the men work. They see what the men do as gifts for them, and so, in the Land of Marriage, do the men intend it to be. When the men look upon the women preparing a meal, their hands dusty with flour, or adding to a celebration the dashes of care and grace that the men would not have conceived in a hundred years of blueprints, they are grateful indeed. It pleases them, it abashes them; they see what the women do as gifts for them, and so do the women intend them to be, and in the Land of Marriage, if there is rivalry between the sexes, it is like the merry raillery of brothers and sisters.

The Land of Marriage is like the secret garden that the girl in the story discovered and tended with care, and "gave" to the local boy who understood plants and growing things, and they then both share it with the crippled heir, and the father who had abandoned that garden when he lost his wife returned to the world of the living. In the Land of Marriage, even a child knows that happiness can only be found by giving oneself away. In other lands, people live in abandoned houses, even rich people; and all around such places, hard, sterile, blank, old but not wise, there is hardly a sign of any such brave surrender. In other lands, flowers must serve a purpose. In the Land of Marriage, purposes must serve the flowers.

The Land of Marriage is enlivened by a love of beauty. I see in that land a boy lying upon his back on the green grass, gazing up into the unimaginable sky. For who in his most fantastic dreams could ever have conceived of the sky? Why is he not poring over his books so as to become sour, harried, wealthy, and divorced? The sky is not for work; we work so that we may look at the sky. He is not old enough yet to be astonished by the beauty of a girl. He will be, though. And it may happen sooner than he knows, because a girl with eyes like the hour before the dawn has just turned the corner and has seen him.

In the Land of Marriage, people don't buy showy things. They make beautiful things. Only someone in love can do that, and the Land of Marriage is filled with such people. There's a man whittling away at a nightstand for his wife, carving out flowery designs in the corners of the drawer, just because they delight him and he knows they will please her. She is knitting a sweater for him, and she's going to put a band of red around the collar, just because that color suits him well, handsome thing that he is.

In nearby Divisia, you cannot enter a public place without being harassed by noise. Ugly thumping rhythm, grunted obscenities, lewd and selfish longings wailed out as by a feral cat; everything harsh and bitter, everything needled and pricked into motion by a relentless avarice; you must have this, you must snatch that, you must seize her, you must seize him, you must fling them away when they are empty or used up and good for nothing. The Land of Marriage is not like that. In the Land of Marriage, it's common to see a teenage boy sitting upon a bench in a park or on a public street, playing a mandolin and singing love songs that his parents and his grandparents sang, while boys and girls gather around, and older people, too.

In the Land of Marriage, there isn't any public lewdness, and that is why there are a lot of public displays of affection. These are simple and childlike, like holding hands and kissing. There's an old man and woman walking down the street, eating ice cream cones and holding hands. People like to go dancing, too, and that is for young and old, and the youngsters look on and shout their approval and clap their hands as grandma and grandpa show them what it really means to trip the light fantastic.

In the Land of Marriage, people do not smear their walls and their plates with excrement, nor their eyes and their minds with porn. There's a lot of porn in Divisia, along with many helpful tips on "performance." The wives in the Land of Marriage roll their eyes and wonder how kindness and gentleness and good humor can be taught by a magazine. Those among them with tart tongues say that they wonder what's wrong with the men in Divisia, because *their* husbands don't seem to need lessons in the art, thank you!

Children are welcomed in the Land of Marriage. Why should they not be? To marry but not to want children would be like planting a tree and cutting off its leaves, or lopping the heads off the roses when they bloom. It would be like seeking a life without friends. It would be like saying, "No, thank you, I am afraid that joy would disrupt my settled routine." For people in the Land of Marriage do not take themselves so seriously. They don't limit the number of their children so that they can devote themselves the more assiduously to their labor, like shuffling papers from one tray to another, or scraping plaque from the teeth of strangers with bad breath.

In the Land of Marriage, it is said that only man can make a vow, and the vow makes the man. When a sociology professor from Divisia came to study their ways, he asked them how they could possibly make a vow of permanence, when they could not predict what the future had in store. The people looked at him as if he had lost his senses. "But that is precisely why we make the vow," they said, "because we cannot predict what the future has in store!"

People in the Land of Marriage do not pursue happiness. They say that happiness pursues them, and you have to go out of your way to dodge it, by selfishness, stubbornness, pride, envy, avarice, wrath, lust, and the rest of them. They prove that the words of Jesus, that he who would save his life must lose it, reveal their truth even in this world. The quickest path to happiness is to forget yourself and to give yourself away for the happiness of somebody else.

In the Land of Marriage, you know your neighbors, because there are neighbors to know. That's because men and women marry and stay married, and raise families, and before you know it, you are like a star in a great constellation, or a leaf upon a full bough of leaves. In the Land of Marriage, fidelity and not restlessness is the rule, and so you not only know your neighbors, you know their cousins, too. In Divisia, people strive with all their might to make a name for themselves, because no one knows who they are. In the Land of Marriage, you don't have to make a name for yourself. You have three or four of them already: what your mother calls you, what your brothers and sisters and cousins and friends call you, what your children call you, and what your wife calls you.

In Divisia, people take it as an affront that the human race is divided into the two sexes, and that these have certain reliable features. They deny more than Adam. They deny the Adam's apple. In the Land of Marriage, the division is all the sweeter for the union that it promises. Men do more than love women: *they like women*, and women like men. What in Divisia is scorned as "stereotype" in the Land of Marriage is a source of delight, like the green of the grass and the cheerful call of Mr. Cardinal as he courts his lady and they build their nest. Boys and girls in the Land of Marriage learn about their sexes just as they learn how to talk and how to use their arms and legs. Parents would no more set about raising a girl to ply a jackhammer than they would teach her to walk about the room on her hands, or to speak without consonants. People in Divisia sneer at them for being old-fashioned, but fashion rules everything in Divisia and very little in the Land of Marriage. If you want to know where Divisia is going to be in five years, all you have to do is to look at the fashions peddled by advertisers and teachers and sex hucksters and television personalities. If you want to know where the Land of Marriage is going to be in twenty years, all you have to do is to look at where it was twenty years ago.

In the Land of Marriage, an old man is taking his grandson fishing, while the boy runs along with him barefoot, and a beagle follows along in doggish delight. The old man can do that, because he never left his wife, and his son never left his wife, and all the bonds of love have been preserved.

In Divisia, there are many more houses than homes. That structure standing in splendid isolation is where the Smiths eat and sleep, and do almost nothing together. If you knock at the door, you aren't likely to get an answer. If you do get an answer, it will be accompanied with a look that says, "We don't want any. Get lost." In the Land of Marriage, there are many more homes than houses. That's because everybody has several homes—their own, and all the others where they are welcome at any time, for any reason. Because people take themselves lightly in the Land of Marriage, and because there are homemakers to make homes and husbands bound to their houses, you don't even bother to knock at the front door. You walk around back and call out, "Gertie, my gal, where's that man of yours!"

There sure are a lot of prudes in Divisia. They don't see themselves that way, but so they are. If a little boy kisses a little girl, they'll hustle him off to the principal and maybe call the police. In the Land of Marriage, they smile, because little boys are apt to do those sorts of things. Innocence clears the field for innocence. In Divisia, people seem to be downright obsessed with sex, and deeply dissatisfied, so that men have nothing good to say about women and women have nothing good to say about men. In the Land of Marriage, people are too busy living to indulge themselves in that hobby. They don't want their men and women neutered, either. What would be the fun in that?

There are as many sinners in the Land of Marriage as there are human beings. But they call sin what it is. They have to, because otherwise there could never be any real forgiveness. People in the Land of Marriage say that there's no similarity between forgiveness and indifferent permission. It's like the difference between giving someone a gift you've thought about for a long time and maybe even cracked your knuckles to make, just because you love him, and giving someone a gift so that he'll think better of you. That last is a kind of bribe, as when parents try to compensate for ignoring their children by showering them with expensive presents they don't need and probably don't want.

The Land of Marriage is a land of giving and forgiving. "It is better to give than to receive," said Jesus, and that's no piece of sentimentality. It is a law of being. Its truth is inscribed upon the human race, in the sexes. The man is for the woman and the woman for the man: each sex is complete only in the other. That's why, in the Land of Marriage, people don't wait for twenty years for the "right" spouse to come along. That makes little sense. Oh, they know quite well the glorious flights of young love! It's just the narrow-eyed list-checking they don't approve. Since they know that they are all sinners and fools, they know that anyone they marry is going to be a sinner and a fool, too, and that instructs them in generosity and forbearance. And gratitude! In the Land of Marriage, the newlywed says, "How good this life is! How wonderful that I've found someone who is far more worthy to be loved than I am, and who puts up with all my faults!" In Divisia, the faults are always on the other side.

In the Land of Marriage, teaching children about what it means to be a husband or a wife, a father or a mother, is the happy work of a lifetime, and in one way or another everybody is engaged in it. About the mysterious secrets of the marriage bed, they speak in private to their children, and that doesn't take long. In Divisia, there are no secrets, nothing is mysterious, everything is vulgarized and splayed out. Sexual "instruction" in school takes years, but as for teaching children about marriage, that never happens at all.

What do we do in the case of the unhappy marriage? That happens too in the Land of Marriage. He drinks too much. She nags. He ignores her and spends too much time at work or with his friends on the golf course. She spoils the children and huddles them to herself. They can't stand one another, and quite often for good reason, as many of their friends and neighbors could tell stories, and have complaints about them of their own. But a vow is a vow. People in the Land of Marriage believe that many such difficult people will grow up, but if they don't, they still must keep their vows, which at the least will require them to keep their troublesome natures to themselves, rather than setting them free like cancerous cells, to spoil second families and third families.

Every ten years or so, a man in the Land of Marriage runs off with another woman, or a woman runs off with another man. These are regarded in the same way you'd regard someone who turned his guns against his countrymen in the battlefield, or someone who stole funds from his business partner to give them to his rival, to help to ruin the business or to swallow it up. Such things stretch their capacity for forgiveness to the utmost. It is far easier for them to forgive a man who burns down a house than a man who burns down a home. But the abandoned spouse receives all of the property and custody of the children. The people do not believe in adding injury to injury.

In Divisia, chills of terror run down the spines of parents who fear that their daughter may fall in love with a boy before she graduates from Yale. When they learn that she cares nothing for the boy she is sleeping with, and that she has flooded her system with the requisite poisons to ensure, as far as can be done, that no child is made, their fears are relieved. In Divisia, love is a feeling, and mere feelings cannot be allowed to get in the way of more important matters, such as the amassing of wealth and the seizing of power. In the Land of Marriage, love is attended by a great many feelings—delight, rapture, sorrow, contentment, longing, gratefulness—but it transcends them all. In the Land of Marriage, love is an act of the will, which creates a bond and a commitment that a mere feeling can only hint at. For feelings are like the weather; but love is like the good, solid earth beneath.

Divisia builds shopping malls, massive sports arenas, institutional schools, industrial plants, government offices, and prisons. The clock rules the world, yet the people are always strangely late for everything, and have a harried and hunted look as they sit in their seats in the subway or the train, no one speaking to anyone near. In the Land of Marriage, the sun and the rain are more important than the clock. That has to be so, because the Land of Marriage is a land of children, and children are not made to obey the rules of the clock. They are hardly made to obey the rules of the sun and the rain.

In Divisia, the word "culture" is still used, for want of a better one, but the reality no longer exists. That's because the people have severed themselves from both the past and from the faith that gave life to their culture. They are like a great tree whose biggest root has been cut. They still derive some nourishment from a few secondary and tertiary roots, but the whole is dying. Most of the poetry and art of their language has become incomprehensible to them, or forgotten entirely. They have lost the Story. In the Land of Marriage, the Story of faith, the Story of hope, and the Story of love are still cherished and are told and retold in a thousand ways, each one as unique and as fascinating as a human face. The Land of Marriage has a culture.

In Divisia, the hands on the clock move their inexorable way towards dead midnight. They tick, tick, and there is no meaning to it, nothing beyond the moment's pleasure or pain. The grandmother lies in a hospital bed, her arms fed glucose by a machine that goes tick, tick, and the morphine that has submerged her in a coma and that will cause her to stop breathing, that too comes from a tube and a machine that goes beep, beep, and a couple of loved ones wait nearby, glancing up at the television now and again, waiting it out, reckoning the number of days required for the dying and the funeral arrangements. They have a vacation planned. So have they lived, and so do they die.

In the Land of Marriage, when a man and woman give themselves each to the other, as long as they both shall live, till death do them part, it isn't just a ceremony, and the vow isn't just a quaint old sentence. The marriage of the man and woman harks back to that of their parents and their grandparents before them. The whole history of mankind is present there, at that hour, in the church, and the people feel it to be so. That young mother with the wiggly little boy whose eyes are hers and whose curly hair is his father's—she testifies to it. The old woman whose wrinkles are like a map of all the joys and the grief she has seen in her life, who remembers now when she and her man were young, and when their first child kicked in her womb, she testifies to it. So does her husband, whose body was laid to rest in the churchyard nearby, twenty-two years ago; he and the white markers rakishly leaning this way and that with the slow shifting of the land, they testify to it, too.

When that man and that woman utter the life-giving promise, they orient themselves toward all the setting suns that ever were, and all the rising suns that shall be. That is because they give their lives to give life, and their promise to be true to one another, come what may, means more than that they will accept the indefinite. It means that they are open to the infinite.

For they do not know what life may spring from their loins, and who the children of their children shall be. They are a chapter in a story they have received and not made, and whose end they will not see in this world. It's a small church with a small spire, surrounded by privet and rosebushes and stands of lilies—the most domestic thing in the world, and therefore the most adventurous thing in the world.

In the Land of Marriage, people cast their seed in a seedbed to grow and bring fruit. That is what life itself is like—the true life. The smallest of all the seeds is sown, and it brings forth the child, and of such is the Kingdom of God.

In the Land of Marriage, no one is so mercurial or so removed from solid, sweet, ordinary reality as even to conceive of marriage apart from a man and a woman, for one another in their manhood and womanhood. That is not because their imaginations are narrow. It is because their intuitions are profound, nor do they have to speak about those intuitions. To see the reality of marriage is like seeing that the vault of the night sky above you is beautiful and deep. People who lack a flair with words can see it as well as the poet can. It is only people whose intuitions have been stunted, and who have grown numb to the beautiful, who will call for an argument about it.

For the Land of Marriage is the marchland of the Kingdom of God, as time is the foreword of eternity. And when the bells ring out joyously in the Land of Marriage, some among the worshipers may look to the skies, as if the bells could bear the heavens away by storm, and when the petals cast in celebration fall upon the wedded couple as they leave the church, I believe I see the faint and shimmering image of a city of peace, descending from heaven as a bride adorned for her bridegroom. Behold, the dwelling place of God is with men; and they are home.

About the Author

Anthony Esolen is Professor of English at Providence College and the author of *The Politically Incorrect Guide to Western Civilization, Ironies of Faith,* and *Ten Ways to Destroy the Imagination of Your Child.* He is also the translator of the celebrated three-volume Modern Library edition of Dante's Divine Comedy (Random House). Esolen holds a Doctorate in Renaissance English Literature from the University of North Carolina at Chapel Hill. He is a Senior Editor for *Touchstone: A Journal of Mere Christianity,* and his articles appear regularly in *First Things, Catholic World Report, Magnificat, This Rock,* and *Latin Mass.*

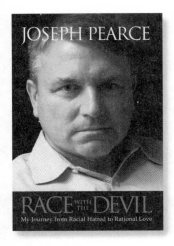

Abandoned ▶

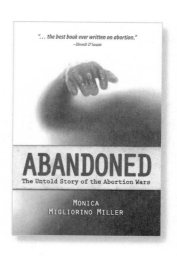

The Untold Story of the Abortion Wars

Monica Migliorino Miller

Every day, thousands of children—fragile, innocent, alone—are abandoned. They are brutally snuffed from the world and literally left in the trash . . . and it's all legal. *Abandoned: The Untold Stories of the Abortion Wars* is the profound, breathtaking, and often daring journey of one woman, but it is much more than that. It is a history of the Pro-Life movement since *Roe vs. Wade*, a suspenseful, true-life tale of life and death, an insightful look into the unique and terrible horror of abortion, and a plea for the protection of the most helpless and innocent members of the human family. *336 pgs.*

978-1-61890-394-5 Hardcover

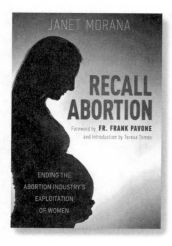

◀ Recall Abortion

Ending the Abortion Industry's Exploitation of Women

Janet Morana

In Recall Abortion, author Janet Morana exposes the myriad ways abortion exploits women, and calls for a national recall of this deadly procedure. She documents the way abortion risks and degrades women's health. And she exposes the false promises and lies by which it is pushed and sold.

978-1-61890-127-9 Hardcover

Dante's Inferno

A Study on Part I of *The Divine Comedy*

Anthony Esolen, Ph.D.

Just as Dante needed Virgil to lead him through the bowels of Hell, you also need a true and trustworthy guide. Dr. Anthony Esolen serves as your Virgil in this course on the Inferno, the first canticle of the Divine Comedy.

Course No. C502

Anthony Esolen, Ph.D.

With Professor Esolen you will enter the terrible gates of Hell and progress level by infernal level to its diabolical depths. Professor Esolen places a special emphasis on the drama of the poem, leading you through each canto in succession. Along the way, he will highlight Dante's astonishing human and theological insights and discuss the destiny of man, how to find our way out of the wilderness of sin, the relationship between love and knowledge, and the integral unity between body and soul.

EIGHT LECTURES
(30 MINUTES PER LECTURE)

DVD Set	$89.95	$69.95
Video Download	$69.95	$59.95
Audio CD	$59.95	$49.95
Audio Download	$39.95	$29.95

CATHOLIC COURSES is an innovative approach to capturing and delivering the riches of our Catholic intellectual heritage. We partner with the best professors and scholars of the Church today, to deliver relevant, faithful courses in HD quality audio and video series.

ORDER TODAY: 800.437.5876   WWW.CATHOLICCOURSES.COM

CATHOLIC
COURSES
Learn More

Dante's Purgatory

A Study on Part II of *The Divine Comedy*

Anthony Esolen, Ph.D.

We know what happens in Hell . . . but what about Purgatory? In this second part of The Divine Comedy, Dante probes the mysteries of that strange and often misunderstood place between earth and Heaven.

Course No. C503

Virgil and Dante discover the astonishing spiritual reality of Purgatory as they climb through the terraces on Mount Purgatory. Dante created a poetic vision which might be the best imaginative representation of Purgatory ever written. While his poem might not reflect the actual nature of Purgatory, his insights can help us understand it better. A celebrated translator and teacher of Dante, Professor Esolen interprets and describes the rich theological insights discovered by Dante on his journey up the mountain.

COMING SOON

Dante's Paradise

A Study on Part III of *The Divine Comedy*

Anthony Esolen, Ph.D.

EIGHT LECTURES
(30 MINUTES PER LECTURE)

DVD Set	$89.95	$69.95
Video Download	$69.95	$59.95
Audio CD	$59.95	$49.95
Audio Download	$39.95	$29.95

CATHOLIC COURSES is an innovative approach to capturing and delivering the riches of our Catholic intellectual heritage. We partner with the best professors and scholars of the Church today, to deliver relevant, faithful courses in HD quality audio and video series.

ORDER TODAY: 800.437.5876   WWW.CATHOLICCOURSES.COM